Growing Up On The Farm

Henry Skupin

Growing Up On The Farm

◆

History in my Lifetime
In Rosebud, Texas
In the 1940's and 1950's
As remembered by the Author

Henry Skupin

iUniverse, Inc.
New York Lincoln Shanghai

Growing Up On The Farm

History in my Lifetime
In Rosebud, Texas
In the 1940's and 1950's
As remembered by the Author

iUniverse books may be ordered through booksellers or by contacting:

iUniverse
2021 Pine Lake Road, Suite 100
Lincoln, NE 68512
www.iuniverse.com
1-800-Authors (1-800-288-4677)

Because of the dynamic nature of the Internet, any Web addresses or links contained in this book may have changed since publication and may no longer be valid.

The views expressed in this work are solely those of the author and do not necessarily reflect the views of the publisher, and the publisher hereby disclaims any responsibility for them.

ISBN: 978-0-595-44047-4 (pbk)
ISBN: 978-0-595-88370-7 (ebk)

Printed in the United States of America

In memory of my Mother and Dad—Hattie and Emil Skupin.

However, the impetus for writing the book was to leave a record of a period that was amazingly different from today for our five grandchildren, Gillian, Kayla, Sebastian, Cecilia, and Gabriel.

Picture on cover—Robert Skupin playing with his Western Flyer little red wagon—1939

Contents

Growing Up On The Farm

Acknowledgements

Special thanks to my wife Anne who spent many hours helping a poor dyslexic farm boy try to write a few sentences that made sense to those of you reading this book. Without her it would have never gotten out of the starting blocks.

To my brothers and their wives', Bob and Janis Skupin and David and Sharon Skupin for supplying me with information I did not know and correcting what I thought I did know. Extra thanks to Sharon who grew up on a farm and was able to fill in information that a farm girl was more familiar with than a little boy. Sharon also was vital in providing most of the pictures via her role as the volunteer family archivist.

To the others like Dale Morrison who said more, more, more detail. For Carolyn Albert's confidence that I could do this and make it interesting to others. For Pat Patton and his attention to detail and his fearless suggestions about rewriting mangled text. My cousin, Rosemary Engel Bell, and my childhood neighbor, Patricia Wimberly Runcie, helped me reach the second of many revisions way back when the manuscript was still on life support.

Help with both ideas and pictures also came from Charlie and Jodie Skupin, Glen and Martha Dodd, Lonnie Dodd, Ann Green Wiggington, Bill Tarver, and Lisa Skupin. Thanks also to Tom Kirkscey and Melvin (Cotton) Wright, who gave me local information gleaned from living most of their lives in Rosebud and who know everything about everybody within 20 miles of town.

A special thanks to our daughter Rebecca Skupin Marcontell, for editorial suggestions, and our son Henry Skupin II, who did a wonderful job with designing the front cover and processing all of the pictures.

The help and encouragement came from four states and three countries. Thanks guys. I could never have done it without you.

And last but not least, thanks to John Sommers for the quote on the front cover:

Thank God I'm A Country Boy

Satellite Map - Skupin Farm
(Note Briary in Upper Right Hand Corner)

Preface

Why in the world would I view a time as recently as the 1940's and 1950's as history? I believe you will appreciate that I have written about hundreds of things that I have personally experienced that will never be experienced by most Americans … ever again. In the days of my youth, there were thousands of people who lived and worked on the farms. With the development of bigger and more sophisticated machines, fewer and fewer farmers were able to work ever increasing amounts of land. This increase in efficiency of farmers caused a massive exodus of people from the farming communities to the cities. The childhood experiences of our current senior citizens who grew up on farms are now part of our rich American history.

My memories are about growing up on a farm in Central Texas near Rosebud in the 1940's and 1950's. Rosebud is located 130 miles South of Dallas on US Highway 77. It is located close to Waco, Temple, and Cameron. The Brazos River is 15 miles East of town. The population of Rosebud is about 1,600 today, which is similar to the number of people who lived there when I was a child. The number of people living in the country, however, was hugely larger back then.

Everything in this book actually happened. Now I was just a child when I had most of these experiences so when I say *"As Remembered by Henry Skupin"* that does not necessarily mean my recollection is 100% accurate. Many people provided ideas and suggestions for this book but any factual errors are mine alone.

You will notice that I am a numbers person and I have used a lot of numbers in describing sizes, weights, and distances. Some of these like the six miles distance from the farm to Rosebud are relatively accurate. Others are guesstimates and may or may not be exact. Remember 43% of all statistics are made up on the spot—including this one.

List of characters:

Robert and Mary Bigler Engbrock—Maternal Grandparents
    Hattie Engbrock Skupin—My mother
    Clara Engbrock Hauk—Mother's sister
        Jim Hauk—Clara's husband
        Children—Katherine and Mary Virginia
    Len Bigler—Grandma Engbrock's brother

Henry and Agnes Reznicek Skupin—Fraternal Grandparents
    Emil Skupin—My father
    Henry Skupin—Dad's brother—Died from a tumor at age of 17
    Tillie Skupin Engel—Dad's sister
        Charles Engel—Tillie's husband
        Children—Rosemary, Peggy, and Gene
    Frank Skupin—Dad's brother—died of dehydration at age one
    Charlie Skupin—Dad's brother
        Jodie Chisholm Skupin—Charlie's wife
        Children—Mike, Janie, Jill, John, and Tim
    Amy Skupin—Dad's sister—Stillborn
    Mary Skupin Surovik—Dad's sister
        Bill Surovik—Mary's husband
        Children—Bruce, Howard, and Amy
    Charlie Reznicek—Grandmother's brother

Robert (Bob) and Janis Smith Skupin—My older brother and his wife
    Children—Steven and Stephanie
Henry and Anne Tonkin Skupin—Author and his wife
    Children—Rebecca and Henry II
David and Sharon Lucko Skupin—My younger brother and his wife
    Children—Lisa and James

Classmates
Billy Allen—From Briary—6 years older than me
John Allen—Briary & Rosebud classmate—1 year older than me

Bea Baca—Rosebud classmate—1 year younger than me

Mike Baca—Bea's brother—about 3 years younger than me

Marvin Bernson—Cousin—Rosebud classmate—one year older than me

Charles Henson—From Briary—7 years older than me

Butch Hauk—Uncle Jim's nephew—Went on vacation with us and got sick

Patrick James—Rosebud & Aggie classmate—1 year younger than me

Mary Lou Lierman Garrett—Rosebud classmate

    Corrie Lierman—Mary Lou's mother—worked in the school cafeteria

Donald Wayne Lewis—Briary & Rosebud classmate

David McAtee—Rosebud classmate

Jackie McCollum—Rosebud classmate

    Julia McCollum—Jackie's mother—Worked in the school cafeteria

Alton McNew—Rosebud classmate

Robert Ocker—Rosebud classmate—1 year younger than me

Billy Pattillo—Rosebud classmate—1 year younger than me

David Repka—Rosebud classmate

Marvin Spivey—Rosebud classmate

Eddie Swanzy—Rosebud classmate

John Tarver—Rosebud classmate

Lois & Louise White—Twins from Briary—5 years older than me

A. D. Whitfield, Jr—Rosebud Wilson High graduate—football star

Patricia Wimberly Runcie—Briary neighbor & Rosebud classmate—1 year younger than me

Delores Wunch—Rosebud classmate

Anton Zucha—Rosebud classmate

Adults

Coach Barkemeyer—UIL Accounting coach

Mrs. Barnes—1st grade teacher in Briary

Cris Davis—Rosebud blacksmith

Vicente Garcia—Worked for Dad as farm laborer

    Children—Jessie and John—Played with me on the farm

H B Halbert—Rosebud Doctor

Judge Haley—Store owner in Lott
Nollie Henson—Briary farmer
Mose Hill—Hauled dead farm animals away
    Head of Rosebud Police after I moved away
Coach Hoelcher—Jr High & Little League coach
R. C. Jackson—Rosebud FFA teacher
Bill Johnson—Ran the VFW Hall
Tom Kirkscey—Owned Rosebud meat locker and movie theater
Jerry Lanicek—Boyhood friend of Dad and Uncle Charlie
Ed Lierman—Drove the Briary school bus route
Alvin Lueke—Boxed against Uncle Charlie
Monroe Parcus—Bookkeeper for Wolf & Son cotton gin
Miss Pendergrass—High school English teacher
Ed and Mildred Slovcek—Neighbors I hitched ride with to Little League practice
George Stock—Lumberyard manager
Mrs. Stubbs—High school English teacher
Donald Thweatt—Rosebud city marshal
Happy Jack Swepston—Rosebud Doctor
Frank Thompson—Worked for Dad as farm laborer
LaDainian Tomlinson—Born near Rosebud—NFL star
Clarence Wolf—Owner—Wolf & Son cotton gin
Gable Zipperlen—Owner of Rosebud Feed and Grain

Big Black Pot and Rub Board

Introduction

The other day I got the following email from a friend. It led me to think about my life as a youth and the many ways it was different from my grandchildren's life today in 2007.

WASHING CLOTHES RECIPE—imagine having a recipe for this!!!

Years ago an Alabama grandmother gave the new bride the following recipe.

This is an exact copy as written and found in an old scrapbook—with spelling errors and all. Author unknown

Build fire in backyard to heat kettle of rainwater. Set tubs so smoke wont blow in eyes if wind is pert. Shave one hole cake of lie soap in boilin water.

Sort things, make 3 piles; 1 pile white, 1 pile colored, 1 pile work britches and rags.

To make starch, stir flour in cool water to smooth, then thin down with boiling water.

Take white things, rub dirty spots on board, scrub hard, and boil, then rub colored don't boil just wrench and starch.

Take things out of kettle with broom stick handle, then wrench, and starch.

Hang old rags on fence.

Spread tea towels on grass.

Give the kids a good scrub down in the wrench water tub.

Pore wrench water in flower bed. Scrub porch with hot soapy water. Turn tubs & kettle upside down.

Go put on clean dress, smooth hair with hair combs. Brew cup of tea, sit and rock a spell and count your blessings.

Oh—For you non-southerners—wrench = rinse.

Growing Up On The Farm

Sausage Stuffer, Sprinkle Bottle
Meat Grinder,Wash Tub & Rub Board

History Lesson #1.
Washing Clothes

After reading the recipe for washing clothes, I immediately saw that an important step had been left out! ***First you had to kill the hog.*** Why? Well, you didn't have lye soap without lard. And the lard came from the hog.

Killing and butchering a hog was an exciting, nonstop full day's work. Done in the fall or early winter, the air would be brisk and everyone would be ready early for a long and yet, rewarding day. It was hard work. But when the day was done we would have prepared several months worth of meat.

> A country boy observation: Few city kids ever experienced this kind of rewarding work. It would be obvious to everyone that my cousins from Dallas were "city kids" but unless it was pointed out most people might be unaware that kids who lived in small towns seldom had these types of experiences either. *"Even if you lived within the city limits of Rosebud, as opposed to on a farm, you might also be a city kid."*

Now let's get back to butchering the hog. First my dad would shoot it in the head so it would die instantly. Then he would cut the hog's throat to drain the blood, which was necessary so as not to spoil the meat. Even the dogs would get excited about what was going on at this point. Dad would drag the carcass onto a homemade sled and use a tractor to pull it over to the tractor shed where we could all work on it together.

Boiling water from the Big Black Kettle (remember the black kettle—it will resurface often) was poured on the dead hog to soften the skin and helps loosen the hair. This made it possible for us to take a knife and scrape off all of the hair from the hog because the skin was left on many cuts of meat. Then the hog was hoisted into the air—head down, where it could be cut open and the guts removed.

The hog's intestines had to be saved and washed out thoroughly so they could be stuffed with the ground up pork scraps to make sausage. Washing and cleaning the intestines without punching a hole in them took careful handling and a good bit of time. That was above my skill level and was done by either Mom or Grandma.

At the same time this was going on Dad was butchering the hog. The edible parts of meat such as hams, pork chops, and roasts were cut, wrapped, and taken to the meat locker in town where they would be kept frozen until we brought them home to eat. Dad would save the raw slabs of bacon for Mother who would cover them generously with salt and place them into a big crock. Then she would fill the crock with water until the salt water covered the bacon. The bacon was preserved in the brine until it was ready to be cooked. We might not eat all of the bacon for several months. The crock was kept out in the chilly breezeway.

During the day, I would be running back and forth between Mom and Dad, doing small chores for each of them. As Dad was cutting up the hog he would save all of the meat scraps to go into the sausage. I might carry these scraps to Mom or just watch what was going on while waiting to be given a job to do. I was the "gofer" on hog butchering days.

Next Mom put the pork and fat for the sausage through a hand cranked meat grinder, which ground it to a consistency similar to hamburger meat. Then she added salt, pepper, and spices for seasoning, mixing it all together well. If I told you what spices she used I'd just be guessing. After all I was just a 10 year old boy. Usually Mother cooked without using a recipe. She would say she did it "by guess and by golly." There was a special device to fill the intestines (now called casings) with the sausage. Mother would carefully place the casings on the greased sausage stuffer tube and then guide the filled casings as I slowly pulled the handle that forced the ground sausage into them. The sausage ends were tied off about every 18 inches making one link. This was repeated until all the ground sausage meat was used. The links were hung from broomstick handles laid across the smokehouse rafters where they would be smoked for a couple of days to give them a distinctive flavor.

Dad carefully saved the remaining fat, putting it into that big black kettle. Then the fire would be stoked up to cook down the fat to "render" the lard. Part of the rendered lard was saved in a five-gallon tin container for use in cooking and baking. And of course we never threw away bacon drippings. The drippings were kept in a coffee can on the back of the kitchen stove and used to add flavor to just about everything Mom cooked.

Finally, we could make the lye soap by boiling the rest of the lard with lye (in that big black kettle) until we had the correct consistency for soap. The hot soap was poured into a wooden apple crate to cool and harden and was only used to wash clothes.

Do you know how you cut the crate-sized hunk of lye soap into pieces? One end of a piece of copper wire was wrapped around a 6 inches long stick. The other end of the wire was wrapped around a second stick. The wire was placed around the block of soap and the sticks, which were handles, were used to pull the wire through the soap to cut it into pieces. I would hold the block of soap while Mom pulled the wire through it. This was repeated until all of the soap was cut in to hand size bars of soap.

Monday was washday. But before Mom began to wash clothes, she would put on a pot of beans that would be the main dish that we ate for lunch. After that she built a fire out in the back yard under that big black kettle (in this case it was called the wash pot), filled it with water, and added about one bar of lye soap sliced into slivers. This soap would remove the skin off your hands if you handled it carelessly. Mother would throw the clothes into the wash pot and punch them with a stick to agitate them. She took them out and *wrenched* them in a number 3 washtub just like the lady's recipe in the introduction described. And Mom did use the word *wrench* for rinse.

Sometimes Mother would have to soak our filthy work clothes in kerosene to break down the grease before she would hand-wash them on a rub board and put them into the wash pot with the lye soap. One thing that made this necessary was that every machine on the farm required lubrication for every moving part. There was no such thing as a sealed bearing that was lubricated for life. Dad and my older brother Robert used a grease gun to pump grease into Alemite grease fittings. (For instance, the two row Allis Chalmers combine had about 70 Alemite fittings, which had to be attached to the grease gun, one at a time, so the bearings could be lubricated each day.) A five gallon bucket of grease was always nearby and was used to refill the grease gun when needed. Using a grease gun was a messy job; sometimes you got as much grease on yourself as in the fitting, especially when the grease gun was refilled by a small boy.

Since the washing machine had moving parts, it also had to be greased before you could wash clothes. Later on Humble (now Exxon) invented Varsol, which was less of a fire hazard than kerosene. Then we used it to clean grease off of everything including our hands. We used so much of it, Dad kept a 50-gallon barrel of Varsol by the tractor shed.

By the time I was 10, sealed bearings had been invented and Dad no longer had to grease all those moving parts on each machine every day. The grease was sealed into the bearing at the factory and often lasted for the life of the machine. This made washing clothes a lot easier since Dad and we boys didn't get covered in grease every day. "The times they were a changing."

Later we got an electric Maytag clothes washer with an agitator, a ringer and two rinse tubs. We still didn't have a hot water heater so Mother still boiled the water for the washing machine outside in the black kettle. The ringer was used to squeeze water out the clothes as they moved from one rinse tub to the next. Sometimes I would be the one who ran the clothes through the ringer. When Mother finished washing the clothes and they had been rung out, she hung them on a clothesline to dry. Clothespins were used to attach clothes to the clothesline and except for a windy day, the dry clothes came off that line pretty stiff.

And what is a rub board (also called a wash board in other parts of the country)? Have you ever heard of one? A rub board is about 18 inches wide by two feet tall with a rough corrugated metal surface. First Mother soaked the clothing that was extra dirty or greasy in kerosene or soapy water and then she rubbed the soiled spots up and down against the rub board. A rub board certainly worked better than an agitator in a washing machine but it also took a lot more elbow grease and it was hard on your knuckles.

Our mother did take about a half hour off in the afternoon and read a romance novel, which she loved to do. She had more than earned those minutes of rest since she worked steadily from the time she got up at 6:00 in the morning until about 8:00 in the evening, or even later if she was making a quilt.

One thing that didn't change for years to come was sprinkling and ironing clothes. A sprinkling bottle was filled with water. Our sprinkler bottle had a rose shaped stopper on top with holes in it like in a saltshaker and Mom or Grandma would sprinkle the clothes they were planning on ironing that day, one piece at a time. Each piece of clothing was then rolled up tightly to allow the moisture to dampen the whole shirt, dress, or pair of pants. These bundles would be packed tightly together in something air tight like an enameled metal dishpan to keep the water from evaporating before the clothes could be ironed. A damp tea towel covered the top of the sprinkled clothes.

You had to be a good judge of how much you could iron in a day because the clothes began to mildew if left damp for too long. If this happened they would have to be rewashed the next week and nobody wanted to do the same work twice over. Aunt Jodie quotes one of David's teachers as saying David could come to school cleaner and go home dirtier than any other kid in school.

> Country Boy Cooking Tip: Notice the last thing your mother does to the food she serves before she puts it on the table. When making biscuits and they are almost fully baked, turn the broiler on and place the biscuits near the broiler for the last 45 seconds to get that nice brown crust on top.

Hattie and Emil Skupin
Mom And Dad

History Lesson #2.
Hattie and Emil Skupin

Mother and Dad had three boys. Robert is five years older than I and David is five years younger. Robert, the first son, was named for our maternal grandfather, Robert Engbrock, which was the custom in Mother's family. When Robert went to college he became known as Bob. Following Mother's custom, I was named for my Dad's father, Henry Skupin. Since we lived in the same town as Grandpa, the family has always called me Buddy. David was just a name they liked. Skupin does not follow the pattern of many Czech names and often people are a little puzzled about how to pronounce it. Skupin is pronounced *Scoop' in.*

Our parents were Hattie Engbrock and Emil Skupin. They were about 20 at the beginning of the great depression and it impacted every decision they made for the rest of their lives. In her early 20's Mother worked as a maid in Waco. I think Mom and Dad "kept company" for 9 years because Dad did not think they could afford to get married. Mom was 30 when they finally married. Her younger sister, Aunt Clara, was married and had two children by that time.

When I was about five, my maternal grandmother, Mary Bigler Engbrock, moved in to live with us. Whenever I say Mom did something, I probably should have said Mom or Grandma did it. But Grandma will be covered in detail later. I also need to mention that both of my parents are deceased. Except for Uncle Charlie and Aunt Jodie, all of the older generation in our family has passed away as I write this in 2007.

When Mom and Dad finally got married, they rented a small 50-acre farm across the road from Mother's parents on thirds and fourths. That meant that the landowner got one-third of all the income from grain and one-fourth of all the income from cotton. That was because there was a lot more labor needed to grow cotton. The renter was responsible for most expenses.

Dad supplemented his farm income by driving a gravel truck. At some point he bought a tractor and in order to earn more with his investment he would hire out to plow for Gibson Farms, which was a very large land-owner in the area. I was told that Dad would plow late into the night on his new tractor. If I know anything about my Dad I can tell you he would have been very proud of that tractor! He always worked aggressively to expand his farming business. He worked like a dog, farmed smart and did very well.

But unlike a lot of farmers, Dad didn't feel as if he needed to get up at 5:00 in the morning in order to put in a hard day's work. He slept in until about 6:00 most days. Quitting time was usually about 5:30 in the winter and sundown in the summer. However, until Robert got to be about 12 and took over the evening milking, Dad still had to milk one or two cows by hand after he came home from the fields.

The land my grandparents lived on and the land my parents were living on when I was born were both next to Pond Creek. Some people think that is a funny name for a creek but it is appropriate for Rosebud. I am told that shortly after I was born, there was a very large rain 5 to 15 miles upstream from where we lived and the water came rushing downstream, flooding both farms pretty badly. I believe I was only a few weeks old when the flood occurred and even though our house was more than a quarter of a mile from the creek, there was water under the house from the flood. Dad told me that there were some people fishing in the creek next to our land and when they looked up and saw the flash flood water coming down the creek channel, they just barely had time to escape.

Uncle Jim Hauk, Aunt Clara's husband, farmed Grandma's land after Grandfather Engbrock passed away but nevertheless, she did not have a great deal of money by the time she lived with us. I do know that a few months after I was born Dad wanted to buy the Hensley place in Briary. The bank told him if he could find someone other than the bank that believed in him enough to loan him $320 they would loan him the other $320 he would need for a down payment on the 320 acre farm. Mom and

Dad borrowed the money from Grandma and Grandfather for the down payment on the farm I grew up on—and that David still farms today.

Dad said everybody thought he was foolish to buy such a huge farm and they were all sure he would fail. After all, at that time most farmers didn't have tractors and were still using mules to work about 50 acres. But the USA had just entered World War II and farm products were bringing good prices. Dad was exempt from being drafted because food was considered an essential war product; so by the time the war was over Dad had completely paid for the farm. He worked hard and smart, but it never hurts to have good timing.

Our farm was on the edge of a community known as Briary. Briary was the location of the one-room school I attended in the first grade, a very small Mission Baptist Church and a country store. The land in that part of the state is generally flat with some low rolling elevation changes. The whole area usually gets enough rain for good farming. Briary is six miles southeast of Rosebud toward the Brazos River. Actually only three couples ever lived in the center of Briary when it flourished … and no one lives at that spot today. The store and teacherage have been gone for decades now. The school, church and the tabernacle where we roller skated remain but are in ruins. The tabernacle had a wooden floor and wooden shutters that could be closed all the way around the building. If we raised the shutters by propping them up with boards, we would have a well ventilated skating rink with a smooth wooden floor. On Sunday afternoons, in good weather, people would just show up and go roller-skating. Of course we had to bring our own skates. (I mean what do you expect for free?)

In other words, there is nothing remaining in what used to be the center of Briary but the intersection of two roads. Nevertheless, everyone who lives within about three miles of where the old Briary store stood, still considers themselves as "from Briary," if they are talking to local folks. Today there are only about 6 couples that live in the Briary area but there were probably more than 50 families (with children) who lived and worked on farms in "Briary" in my childhood.

It isn't easy to describe ones parents. I know some people will read this who knew them and they will have opinions that differ radically from mine. But here goes. First, I'm going to tell you what they weren't. They weren't very touchy feely. After we were 4 or 5 they almost never gave hugs. They didn't greet friends with a kiss on the cheek and they never said I love you, however they were fiercely loyal to their three boys and cared for us deeply and we all knew it! So what else were they? Emil and Hattie Skupin were honest to the core, worked hard, didn't lie, didn't drink, didn't smoke and in general were respected by people who knew them. Being respected by those who know you isn't a bad place to start.

They never talked about themselves and I would say most people that knew them probably knew them pretty well, only because what you saw was what you got. My Aunt Jodie once said that we three boys were raised by three of the strongest minded people she had ever known. Then she elaborated—"They just never agreed with each other about anything." She was talking about Mom, Dad and Grandma Engbrock. My Aunt Jodie was no pushover herself. However she married into the family and may have been a bit more open minded than the average Skupin or Engbrock.

I have read that Czechs always liked a good verbal fight. It is said that if three Czechs moved into a community they would start two newspapers. Apparently it is a long-standing part of our culture to argue and disagree. That was true at our house, where the arguments between Mom and Dad could get quite heated. Although their anger was soon forgotten, it was disturbing to me, especially when I lay in bed at night listening to them before I went to sleep. Looking back, I think it was just one of their styles of communication.

Dad was very frugal, but Mother could pinch a penny till it cried "uncle." Besides growing and "putting up" almost all of the food she put on the table, plus working in the fields during harvest times, Mother made all of her clothes, including her pajamas and slips, shirts for us boys, and a quilt or two each year. Of course that doesn't come close to fully describing all that she did because there were three meals a day to prepare, dishes to wash, clothing, sheets and towels to wash, dry and iron, patching, cleaning house, etc, etc, etc. One of the old sayings that Mom used from time to time was, "A man may work to dusk from dawn, but a woman's work is never done."

When I was very little Mother played the accordion once in a while. She didn't play it very often but it was fun to watch her play. I think the accordion is kind of like playing bagpipes because the music is created by squeezing air out of the billows. Mother always kept her Dad's fiddle and hoped that one day one of us boys would take up the violin. Robert played the steel guitar for a couple of years in high school and she had the violin restrung and got David to take a few violin lessons. That was about all of the music interest she was able to squeeze out of us boys. What about me and music? The best decision I ever made was to not take up anything musical. I can't even carry a tune when I hum.

Since Dad was a farmer, he worked on the farm that surrounded our house all day and, except for when we were in school, we almost always ate three meals a day at the kitchen table with the entire family. Dad never did much in the kitchen, except refill the syrup pitcher before breakfast (from the gallon bucket of Karo syrup). Those Karo buckets had many uses after they were emptied. Even today when we point at a Karo syrup bucket and ask our kids what it is, they will reply, "It's a cookie jar." That is an inside joke in our family since that was one prominent use Mom had for the empty buckets.

We all sat down and ate together three times a day and we talked to each other at those meals about what was going in our lives. My folks discussed whatever was on their minds right out in the open, in front of us kids. So everyone knew what was going on and what the adults were concerned about. We boys were allowed to express our opinions even when they were different from the adults. Actually, my Dad played a sort of game with us where he would say something he knew we disagreed with to entice us to argue with him. He was, whether he knew it or not, teaching us to stand up for our own ideas even against adults. I think that was pretty rare, particularly in that day and time.

It has been my experience that people who grew up on farms and in small communities like I did, were given much more trust, freedom and responsibility at an early age than people who grew up in big cities and are more likely to feel that their parents did a good job of raising them. We may not have lived in as big a house or had as many toys or other luxuries as were common in town but we learned a good work ethic and were taught some pretty good fundamentals of leadership—even if fancy words like those were never used. With the exception of Little League in the summer time, we didn't need adults to organize our free time for us. A lot of the time our parents just went outside to work and we followed them out. It was left to us to decide how we would play, be it ride a tricycle, pet a dog, climb a tree, or push a rolling car tire as we ran after it for an hour without stopping.

One story about me that lives in family lore, was that when I was about three my Mother told me to pick up my shoes off the living room floor and put them away. My response was, "I Ain't No Shoe Picker Upper!" Now I know you will find that hard to believe about a sweet little boy like me. Mom picked me up and took my little hands, with me squirming and fighting her and put my little fingers around the shoes and carried me, shoes and all, into my room to put them away. Mom told my wife, Anne, this story one day after Anne asked Mother how she had disciplined her children. When Anne asked what she had done the next time I left my shoes in the living room, Mom answered, "Well, I sure didn't tell him to pick them up!" Personally, I have my doubts about never being asked to pick up my shoes after that.

However, it is obvious my parents did not worry much about minor discipline issues. They did, however, focus strongly on our physical safety. For instance we were firmly and frequently reminded to stay away from the well and the ponds where a child might drown. Whenever we worked with a tractor or tools we were constantly reminded of what to be careful about, in order to avoid injury. Mom and Dad always took the time and effort to remind us about safety over and over again.

When we boys were little, Dad would sometime stretch out on the couch on Sunday afternoon and listen to the Czech Melody Hour on KMIL, the Cameron radio station. Since Dad had grown up speaking Czech at home he always welcomed the chance to hear the Czech language. I would climb up on the couch, get behind him and try to push him off while giggling and laughing. Dad would tickle me to keep me from getting leverage too easily and to keep the game going for a while. He would end up on the floor two or three times each play session. I think he enjoyed the game as much as I did.

When Dad was working, he was single minded about what he was doing. But when he stopped to relax he had a twinkle in his eye and was looking for ways to enjoy himself. Playing with kids was definitely one of the things he enjoyed. If there was a small child around, it was going to be in Dad's arms. Toddlers would be lured over for an ongoing game of poke and tickle. Dad would be grinning from ear to ear as he scooped up youngsters under about four years old, sat them in his lap so they were looking directly into his eyes and he would make his eyebrows dance. It was magical! Small children would get a big quizzical grin and break into a giggle as Dad repeated this several time. He loved to do this with all his grandchildren. What he did was wrinkle his forehead several times and each time that drew his bushy eyebrows up and down. Without exception, small children would grin from ear to ear and reach out for Dad's eyebrows with their tiny hands. Parents always got a kick out of watching Dad play with their kids this way.

Mom, on the other hand, had an excess of nervous energy and was always too busy doing things to stop for more than a few minutes to play with children. What you usually saw of Mom was the back of her head as she disappeared on the way to do another chore. When she cooked a big meal for the entire Skupin clan she would often open the refrigerator after the meal and find something she had forgotten to put on the table. As soon as we started to eat, she would begin to find fault with her own cooking and to apologize for her imagined cooking shortcomings. I say imagined because in fact, she was an excellent cook. Several times during each meal she would jump up and run to the kitchen "to do one more thing." I can still hear Dad fruitlessly saying, "Hattie, sit down!" as she headed for the kitchen again. Mom showed her love by her never-ending efforts to take care of her family.

Another thing Dad did that I found amusing was that he would talk to himself. He would talk out loud about everything he was worried about. Not quite loud enough to be understood, but almost. If he talked aloud when we were almost close enough to hear him, I can only imagine how he must have talked to himself when he was alone driving that tractor for 10 or more hours a day.

Of course, Dad worried about bole weevils and bole worms in the cotton and he worried about rain but there were a lot of other things that could go wrong on a farm. Granted, lack of rain was the one thing that he worried about most but I can remember a few times he had a problem with too much rain. A rainy spell at planting time could prevent him from planting and once a very large rain caused a good bit of our crop to drown out. Also, a hurricane like Carla in 1963 could do a lot of damage to mature cotton and corn crops just when they were ready to be harvested.

A rain when he needed to poison the cotton for insects created another problem since he couldn't get into the muddy fields with his tractor. He would have to hire an airplane out of Cameron to come out and spray the cotton fields. Sometimes, I would be the one to wave a flag (called flagging) for the pilot to line up for his next spraying pass. Once the pilot got lined up on the row he wanted to spray, I quickly moved out of his path over to where he would spray next. Another insect that caused a problem was midge in the maize crop but I don't think we sprayed for that back then. Hail could destroy a crop just as it was beginning to mature and everything could be lost. Although I don't remember a hailstorm that ever totally destroyed our crops, hail did destroy other farmers' crops near us occasionally.

Cows are living creatures and a whole multitude of bad things can happen to livestock. They can eat something poisonous, get out on a public road and get hit by a car, get sick, need to be fed or get a plague like "black leg" and the whole herd would have to be shot and burned. A good worrier can come up with an endless list of things to talk to himself about and Dad could worry with the best of them.

There was a lot of anxiety and uncertainty that went hand in hand with farming. There would come a time in early summer almost every year when Dad would start saying how we needed a rain in the next three days or the crop was going to be lost. It was just getting too late to save it if it didn't rain now. Next week was just going to be too late. I noticed that almost all Skupin crops were miracles because they were successful in spite of the certain failure that Dad had foretold just a few weeks before. Uncle Bill was also known for gigging Dad about his miracle crops. However, there was always the real possibility that rain would not come for a couple of years, as happened in the Oklahoma dust bowl, and the entire farm could indeed be lost. Enough crop failures did occur over the years to keep that possibility alive and well in Dad's mind.

The Skupin family rarely went on a vacation. Before I tell you about our only vacation, a contrast of a road trip from those days with today might be educational. Let's say we wanted to go to Dallas to see Aunt Mary and Uncle Bill. That couldn't be all that different than today. Dallas is only 135 miles from Rosebud, so it probably wouldn't take much more than two hours to get there, right? Wrong!

It probably took close to four hours. First, the speed limit was 60 and second there were no freeways. Roads were built to get you from one town to the next, so the highway went right through the middle of each town. Getting through Waco, Hillsboro, Waxahachie and around Loop 12 in Dallas (it may have been a loop but it had a bunch of traffic lights) took forever. On top of that we had to drive through the middle of a little town like Lott or Chilton every ten miles, all the way to Dallas. If it was summer time it would be hot and we would have all the windows rolled down. Today it isn't obvious but the wind and the noise from the wind, would beat on us the entire way and we would all be exhausted by the time we got to Dallas.

Since cruse control hadn't been invented yet, Dad had to really concentrate. Otherwise he would find himself driving 50 mph one minute and 70 a few minutes later. Also cars didn't have power steering or power brakes, so driving long distances was more demanding even if it was wintertime and the windows were up. Another thing that slowed us down was that most of the roads were two-lane and if Dad wanted to drive faster than someone in front of us, he had to wait for an opening in the oncoming traffic so he could pass safely.

There were no fast food places and we didn't want to take the time or spend the money to stop at a restaurant, so my parents were careful to see to it that they packed a few sandwiches and a little fruit for us. The only place to go to a restroom when we traveled was at a gas station (or behind a friendly bush.) Even gas stations were different from today. They didn't include a convenience store, just a couple of vending machines. They sold gas, had a couple of bays where they did car repairs, and had primitive restrooms by today's standards. We wouldn't need a place to stay overnight on such a short trip but if we had, the motor hotels, i.e. motels, were just being built. Before then an overnight traveler had to stay at a hotel.

When someone went on a trip, they didn't just get in their car and go. Cars weren't as dependable as today, so Dad would check the oil, the radiator, and make sure all the tires had the right air pressure before we left home. All service stations were "full service" back then so when we bought gasoline the attendants would start pumping the gas and then would also check all of these same things Dad had checked as well as wash the windshield. The driver never had to get out of the car because the service station attendants filled the gas tank and did all this checking every time anyone bought gas.

Now back to our vacation. We only went on one vacation the entire time I was growing up. (Actually I didn't know of any farmers that went on vacations.) I was about 11 when we took a trip that targeted Pike's Peak, Seven Falls, the Royal Gorge in Colorado, and Yellowstone National Park in Wyoming as our vacation highlights. But once again we never did anything the simple way. Two other families from Clarkson went with us and we all shoehorned ourselves into two cars. I think there were 11 people packed into a Ford and a Chevrolet. Every possible space in both cars was absolutely crammed with clothing, food and stuff for the trip. I remember we would stop at roadside parks and everybody would make sandwiches for lunch.

Of course the trip did not work out at all the way it was planned. Butch Hauk was a little younger than I was and he had a history of getting sick quite a bit. Sure enough, when we got to Raton Pass, New Mexico, Butch got sick. He spent three or four days in the hospital and while we were there we explored the Raton Pass area during the day. If we were going to get stuck somewhere, Raton Pass wasn't a bad place. I mean it beat Dalhart or Amarillo, for instance.

I had never seen anything higher than a West Texas mesa, or ever been in a forest so Raton Pass was pretty exotic to me. Eventually we did get to Pike's Peak on July 15th. I remember because it was Robert's birthday and it was snowing up on top of the mountain. That trip was the only time I saw a mountain before I was about 26 years old. I think we took the limo up the mountain because we were afraid our cars would overheat. I wonder what happened to that granite rock we brought back from up near the peak? It sat beside our fireplace for many years.

Back when I was in junior high I once had a little trouble sleeping for a couple of nights. At the breakfast table on the third morning Mom asked me how I had slept. I said I just couldn't get to sleep at all. It was awful. I had laid there awake forever. Dad then pointed out I must have gotten a little sleep because he had stood on the back steps and shot a possum with a shotgun about five feet from where I was sleeping next to an open window and I hadn't even stirred. Suddenly the worse case of insomnia in my life was cured.

When I was young we had three dogs: Max, Jeff and Jack. They weren't big dogs but they barked like crazy every time a car drove up and that was exactly what Dad wanted them to do. He probably wished they wouldn't chase cars but why complain about details, right? They lived outside and didn't come in the house but they were well cared for.

Later, Aunt Clara had a female dog named Puddles who had puppies. We got a male puppy from that litter and named him Scamp. Dad had always taken time to pet and even feed our dogs but before Scamp he never allowed a dog to come inside. Scamp quickly broke that barrier. So you could "teach an old dog (Dad) new tricks." Don't misunderstand. Scamp was allowed inside whenever he wanted, but like us boys, he spent most of his time outside because that was where the people were.

Scamp was Dad's dog. If Dad sat in a chair, Scamp was in his lap. If Dad opened the pickup door, Scamp was going to be inside that pickup in a flash. Even though Scamp was short, he was quite sturdy and quick enough to catch rabbits. Whenever we were in the fields driving a tractor, Scamp would come along. I might be shredding cotton stalks, which was noisy, and I think the rabbits would get distracted by the tractor. Scamp would sneak up on them from the downwind side and catch himself another rabbit. He caught many more than I ever came close to shooting, that's for sure. After he caught and killed one, he would be sure to drag it over to where the tractor was working so he could show me (or Dad) what good work he had done.

Dad was concerned because most of the farmers' wives outlived their husbands and even though they weren't ready to retire Mom and Dad built their dream home in town in about 1970. From the new house Mom would be able to walk to the grocery store, to church, to see her friends etc. after he died. (Of course Dad outlived Mom by 12 years, go figure.) Scamp was getting up in years by then. There were a couple of times he disappeared and once he had walked those 6 miles back to the farm. Another time Dad found him on the gravel road about two miles out of town headed for the farm. I guess "you can take the dog out of the farm but you can't take the farm out of the dog."

Dominoes was one of the few games my parents ever played. Actually the game was 42, which was a domino game played by two couples. When three couples were available they played 84, which was a variation played with two boxes of dominoes. 42 is sort of a simplified version of bridge with bidding and trumps. The men would always play against the women and Dad seemed to almost have ESP about what dominoes his partners held. He would often make seemingly impossible bids and then ask his partner if he held a certain domino. If the partner said yes, and he often did, Dad would lay down his hand because it was a clear winner.

Dad only went to school through the 6th grade but it is obvious to me that all of us boys got our math and engineering skills from our father. Mother did complete high school but at that time high school only went through the 11th grade. Both Mom and Dad thought that their boys getting a college education was essential and they sacrificed a lot to see to it that we did. They paid for all of our college expenses and provided each of us with a car while we were in school.

Even with all of the responsibility and trust we were given, we were human and of course we did a few things that upset our parents. I will cover some of these things later like Robert stripping the gears in the car and me backing the truck into the tractor. When we did something wrong, Dad would chew us out at every opportunity for a few days but after that it was seldom mentioned. Don't get me wrong, Mom and Dad didn't forget. They just didn't dwell on our mistakes for very long. Even when my grades may not have been as good as they would have preferred they didn't complain. For example, I made mostly C's my first semester in college and my parents thought it was great that I passed every course. My wife, on the other hand, made all A's except for one B and her father wanted to know what went wrong in that one course (and she knew he meant it.)

Both by their example and by the opportunities they provided us, Mom and Dad taught the three of us to be ethical, confident, independent, value strong family ties, take pride in our work, and oh so much more. When Mother passed away Dad was obviously very distraught and he told us a few things we had never heard before. He said that in 46 years of marriage the only time Mother hadn't been home to sleep in the same bed with him was when she was in the hospital having David. (Robert and I had been born at home.) He mentioned that he had been in the hospital for surgery a couple of times but he couldn't remember any other times they hadn't gone to sleep together at night holding hands.

> Mom's Country Recipe: When making cole slaw, fry some bacon crisp and set aside the bacon to garnish the cole slaw. Then add mayonnaise, vinegar and the bacon drippings to the thinly sliced cabbage. (Do not use that store bought cole slaw dressing.—It is awful!) Season to taste and mix thoroughly. Crumble the bacon into bits to sprinkle on top and dig into the best cole slaw I've ever eaten.

David - Happy as a Pig in Slop

History Lesson #3.
Playing on the Farm

When I was a toddler my big brother was pulling me around inside the house in a little red wagon and took a corner too quickly. The wagon turned over, I fell out and broke the little toe on my left foot. I'm quite sure that is why I was never as good an athlete as the other boys. Once the toe got well it never hurt or anything but there must be some reason I wasn't a better athlete. My reason is that toe—that's my story and I'm sticking to it!

We boys had no playmates to speak of, except for one another. Sure there was one house a little less that a half mile away and they had a couple of kids that were David's age. There were about three other houses within several miles, but they were definitely too far for me to walk over to visit them. We did have a Mexican family named Garcia who worked for Dad and lived in a house on the farm that was provided for them as part of their salary. They had a son named John who was my age and another son named Jesse who was a couple of years older. I played with John a lot and we sometimes played with Jesse.

Discrimination was a matter of fact in those days. I could play outside all I wanted with the boys, but I was not to bring them into the house. I didn't go in their house either. Of course, Mother would give us water to drink or a few cookies if we came to the back door and asked for them. In those days if we were outside and wanted a drink of water we usually just picked up a garden hose, turned on the faucet and drank all we wanted.

Car tires were much smaller than today. John and I would each get an old worn out car tire, run behind it and push it to keep it rolling. We would probably go close to a half a mile from the house even at a very young age, like 6, pushing our tires and running behind them. We would do this for hours each day, in both the morning and the afternoon. John and Jesse moved away a couple of years later and I was back to only having my brothers to play with.

I was allowed to go just about anywhere on the farm, but I was not to go near a cattle stock tank because I could drown. Also, I was warned that if I went into the pasture I needed to be careful if the bull was around. I was told not to run from the bull if he came after me but to let him get close and dodge him. I usually gave the bull a pretty wide berth unless there was an adult around so I never had to test the "dodge the bull theory."

Mom would give each of us an Easter basket a day or two before Easter Sunday and send us out on the road between the house and the mailbox to fill it with grass and Texas wildflowers like bluebonnets, buttercups, and Indian paint brush. Of course the bigger brother was to be sure and help his little brother make a lush Easter basket. The older brother got to help Mother dye and decorate a dozen or more Easter eggs on Saturday afternoon. Mom would hide the colorful eggs and after we found them all we would then re-hide them several times, for a day or two. Part of the fun was to peel and eat as many as we wanted. Sometimes one or two of them wouldn't be found until weeks later when they were good and rotten and those had to be thrown away, of course.

Farmers are always building things and tearing things apart, like building a cotton trailer, or doing a little remodeling on the house. You know, stuff like that. Dad kept a pile of scrap lumber behind the tractor shed and we were free to use it. Since there were no power tools in those days we pretty much had access to all of Dad's tools and could use the lumber to make just about anything we wanted as long as we didn't just cut it up and waste it. That pile of lumber always gave us "potentially something to do."

My brother Robert had built a tree house in a big oak tree in the side yard next to our house. As he got older, the tree house fell into disrepair so when I was about eleven, I decided to rebuild it. Mostly that meant building a new floor. Sure, it was a "tree house," but it wasn't enclosed—just a platform. I was up in the tree sawing off a board in an awkward position when the saw jumped out of its slot and sawed into the knuckle of my left thumb. It was bleeding pretty badly so I went into the house to get something to stop the bleeding. I didn't want my mother to know what I had done but she spotted blood and I had to go to Dr. Sweptson's and get a few stitches and a tetanus shot. Today that scar still reminds me of that tree house way back when.

I erected a safety net around the tree house made with baling wire. To make the net I simply wove the wire so that the platform was surrounded by a net of four-inch squares, which would make it difficult to fall out of the tree house. Since Dad did repairs on machinery under that tree he had pulled an electrical outlet out there. I found an old thrown away electric plug-in and made myself another electrical outlet up in my tree house. I would take a radio from the house into the tree house and listen to Elvis sing "Jail House Rock" and "Love Me Tender." That was before transistors, which meant it was before transistor radios, of course. When kids came over to play, which wasn't all that often, they always got a tour of the tree house. It may not have been much, but it was mine!

We never had many toys. We didn't need them. With Mother working outside so much doing things like planting, hoeing weeds, or harvesting in the garden, washing clothes, plucking chickens, etc., we spent almost all of most days outside. I mean no one had TV's so we couldn't go watch TV or play a video game or stuff like that. We had dirt to dig in, chickens or cats to chase, tricycles to ride and access to all of Dad's tools, lumber, and stuff, so we didn't need toys. We just went outside and figured out a way to get busy. I think we pretty much stayed outside until we were called in to eat or do something for Mom. There just wasn't much to do inside in those days.

We also had a mulberry tree and two pecan trees in our yard and the mulberry tree had a swing hanging from one of the limbs. I would swing so high that I knew if I went any higher I might go over the top of the tree limb upside down. I mean, every kid that has ever been on a swing should know that feeling. I remember David breaking his arm in about the third grade at school. He was swinging standing up on the swing and he jumped out as the swing came forward. I thought about doing that many times but

I don't think I actually tried to do it while swinging way up high. Oh well, farm boys did have a few accidents even if they weren't all on the farm.

We spent a lot of time climbing the mulberry and pecan trees, the higher the better, of course. The mulberries would get worms so you had to be a little careful before you bit into one. But a tree ripened mulberry tasted pretty good and we had an unlimited supply when they were in season. Mom was the only one who even noticed that they left dark stains on our fingers and on our clothes.

The crows loved to steal the pecans from the two pecan trees in the front yard. Every year we would try to catch a crow in the pecan trees and shoot it. Then it would be my job to climb up high in the tree and hang the dead crow there. The other crows tended to stay away if there was a dead crow hanging in the tree. Of course, we boys ate quite a few pecans that we picked up in the yard and cracked with our teeth. We also picked up a bunch of nuts and shelled them (usually with Mom and Grandma) so they could use them in various dishes, including my personal favorite—pecan pie.

We may not have had many toys but we seemed to always have a wagon, our own tricycle and later our own bicycle, even if they were sometimes hand-me-downs. I loved to ride my tricycle, and later my bicycle. I liked to compete but I had no one my age to play with. I did have a little brother, David, who is five years younger than I am. Of course I was supposed to keep an eye on my little brother anyway. And I had a "high quality" Timex watch with a second hand that only lost a couple of minutes a day. The Timex ad said, "It could take a licking and keep on ticking."

So I invented timed bicycle races between David and me. I had to come up with ways where he could win once in a while or he would not play with me. So I would handicap myself, meaning I would take something that took me three minutes to do and give myself a one minute handicap. This way I had to beat David by a minute or he won. I was always quite fair because in this game the objective wasn't so much to win as to keep David involved in playing with me. You do believe that, don't you? So we would ride the bicycle course separately and that good old Timex watch determined who won.

We rode our bicycles often and we rode them hard and fast. I loved to go as fast as I could and jam on the brakes and slide sideways to a stop. I never needed to worry about traffic, falling on hard pavement, or even needing to go down to the park to ride where I would be safe. My entire world was safe.

When David and I ran the timed races in the yard, the course we used was a triangle with that big old mulberry tree in the middle. We had to apply the brakes a lot to make the hard turns. Back in those days brakes were on the foot pedals rather than handbrakes like today. I never understood just how they worked but I do know there was a series of washers with notches on them in the rear axle and we would jam on the brakes so hard that eventually we would chip the corners off of those notches and the pedals on the bike no longer worked properly. Dad would send us into the White Auto store in town where we would buy ourselves a new set of washers.

Then we had to install them. The axle was full of grease and once we finally got the new washers all lined up and installed we had to refill the axle with grease before we put it back together. By the time we finished we would be greasy from head to toe. I suspect there was even grease in our hair. After the bike repairs were completed we washed our hands using some of the Varsol in that 50-gallon barrel and Mother was left to deal with our clothes. The bath didn't come until dark because we would just need another one before bedtime if we took one in the middle of the day.

Farmers are usually crying for more rain, wanting rain in the winter so the soil will be moist down deep when they plant, wanting rain after they plant so the seed will germinate and pop out of the ground, and then wanting rain every couple of weeks all summer. But that isn't the way Mother Nature usually works. The rains tend to stop coming in late spring and as the crops begin to wilt the farmers begin to squirm.

So, except for rain when they are trying to plant or harvest, a rainy day is a day of welcome relief. And the kids knew it, so what did we do after a good soaking rain? We took off our shoes and went walking barefoot in the mud. We had an unlimited supply of mud after a rain. The cool mud would squeeze up between our toes and felt wonderful. When we found a mud hole we just stood in one place and stomped our feet up and down in a small circle until the mud turned into a liquid slurry. We called this making a mud pie and nobody makes a better mud pie than a barefoot farm boy.

One night when I was 10 or 11, I was playing with David when he did something to me and I started chasing him through the house and out into the breezeway. As David ran through the door into the breezeway he slammed the door behind him and the big glass pane in the top half of the door shattered. I didn't know it at the time, but that turned out to be the last time I was spanked. And what about little David? He got off scot-free, of course. Life isn't always fair.

By the age of 14, I was allowed to take a rifle and go hunting in our pasture by myself. There were a lot of strict rules that I had to follow but I was allowed to hunt without supervision. As a youngster I had a Red Rider BB gun and by the time I was 8, I had a pellet rifle so I had done a little shooting. I had also shot a 20 gauge single shot shotgun a few times.

Still, going hunting by myself was big kid stuff. The main rule was to be careful about what was in the background when I was shooting because a 22-rifle bullet would carry a long way. For instance I was not to shoot up in the air because I would have no clue where the bullets would land. Long rifle shells supposedly had a range of one mile and if there were any people or cattle anywhere in the direction I was shooting I was to skip taking that shot. I must admit I don't remember ever actually killing very much. Mostly I hunted rabbits and there were several times I spent a lot of time sneaking up on bushes that had disguised themselves as jackrabbits.

About the same time I was also allowed to go bird hunting with the single shot shotgun. I quickly discovered that the best time and place to hunt doves was at the stock tanks about the last 30 minutes before sundown. Late in the evening the Mourning Doves would come to the stock tanks for water in small flocks and the hunting could get pretty good. If you wanted to hunt birds in the middle of the afternoon you had to walk them up one bird at a time in someplace like a harvested corn patch and you seldom got many good shots doing that. Once again, I fired a lot of shells but really didn't bring home many birds. We did eat what we killed although I don't ever remember Mom cleaning a bird because the "Mother's Union" had designated that as the hunter's job.

Dad had an old 10-gauge shotgun that reached a point it probably wasn't safe to shoot anymore. I was never big enough to shoot it before we quit using it. It had a kick that would just about knock down a grown man and once you shot it a couple of times your shoulder was going to be sore for a few days so I wasn't all that upset that I never got to shoot that big gun. I don't ever remember seeing another 10-gauge shotgun.

Before I got to junior high, the high school boys who lived in our community would get together on Sunday afternoon and "do stuff." Each little community had a softball team and the different teams would play each other. We were from Briary and we might play Clarkson. Briary had a small community store and the Clarkson community had two stores about a mile apart, one of which was owned by my Aunt Clara and Uncle Jim. (My Uncle Charlie and Aunt Jodie owned the other store for a while but I think that store convinced them they needed to leave Rosebud and find a more profitable way to make a living.) The softball competition was fierce but everybody knew everybody so it was also a lot of fun. Unfortunately, by the time I got into high school things had changed and the Sunday sporting competition between communities had dwindled away.

Another thing we did was go swimming. I had only been swimming a few times in my life when I was in junior high school and didn't know how to swim yet. Robert was in high school and he had to take me along on Sunday afternoons. There was a swimming hole in Pond Creek way back off the public road, that was owned by the Allen's, and about ten or more of us Briary boys would show up, take off our clothes, and just go skinny-dipping. I suspect that several of the boys (including me) did not even own a swimsuit. The older boys played a game like "tag—you're it." The guy that was "it" would get in the middle of the creek and the other boys would try to swim across the creek without getting tagged on the head. If the guy swimming across the creek was swimming underwater the one who was "it" had to pull his head above water before he could tag him on the head. The older boys would also dive off of the creek bed into the deepest water.

Have you ever heard of a corncob fight? Corncobs aren't real dense like rocks and we had a ready supply left over from shelling corn daily to feed the chickens. One can get hit pretty hard with a cob and it will sting for a while—but not too long. John Allen and his older brother Billy would sometimes come over on Sunday afternoon and we might end up in the hayloft where we would have a corncob fight. John, who was one year older than me, would team up with me against our brothers who were both five years older than we were. (No, that never seemed all that fair to me either, but we did it anyway.)

Each side would build a fort out of hay bales up in the hayloft and collect a stash of corncobs and we would go at it. Corncobs would go zinging past our heads like crazy. Sometimes we would charge the other side and get in a good hit or two and then run back for cover. It was fun until one of the older brothers hit John or me upside the head or somewhere that hurt like the dickens and we would scream and then quit for the day. John and I always took a beating but we usually managed to get in a few good licks ourselves.

Even with all of the roughhousing we seldom did much damage to ourselves. My sophomore year in high school I was roller-skating in our small garage one afternoon and as I was headed over to the door to take off my skates I slipped, fell, and broke my arm. I wore a cast for quite a while and as it got close to healing I remember using the cast to help me spike a volleyball really hard during recess at school. With two weeks to go in the football season my senior year one of my teammates, Billy Pattillo, blocked me hard with his forearm one day at practice and broke my nose. His forearm must have barely missed my facemask and I didn't get to play in the last two games my senior year. Those two injuries, along with David's arm, were the only broken bones I remember the Skupin boys having growing up.

We loved to make homemade ice cream late in the day, although, I think what we really loved to do was to **eat** homemade ice cream. It was one of the highlights of living on the farm. We had a two and one half gallon ice cream maker. That baby was hand cranked and once I got old enough I had to pitch in and help with the cranking. Turning the crank gets pretty hard once the ice cream mix begins to freeze. When we made homemade ice cream we would fill the metal container 3/4's full with milk, sugar, cream, and vanilla and let the freezing ice cream expand to completely fill it to capacity.

We would place the container inside the wooden tub and then we would add a layer of ice covered by a liberal layer of rock salt in the space between the metal container and the tub. We would turn the crank a little while and then add another layer of ice and salt until the churn tub was full of salted ice all the way to the top. We bought the ice at the icehouse in town, where it cost 15 cents for a 25-pound block of ice, but we had to use an ice pick to chop off pieces small enough to fit into the ice cream tub.

In addition to the size of our ice cream maker, the really big difference between our homemade ice cream and any other you may have eaten was that the milk from our Jersey cows had so much cream in it. We didn't separate any of the cream from the milk we used to make ice cream. Not only that, we actually added extra cream to make the mix really rich. Our ice cream was better than Blue Bell! We would eat a very light supper on days we made ice cream. We might only have a sandwich, and then we would eat ice cream until the world looked level. We probably would get the first bowl about 6:30 or 7:00 in the early evening and we might get our last bowl about 9:45.

My Uncle Charlie told me that when he and Dad were little they made homemade ice cream one day and there was a little left in the churn so he woke up about midnight and snuck in to get one more bowl. But he said Dad had beaten him to it and all that was left in the ice cream maker when he got there was a little puddle in the bottom. Yes, life on the farm was tough! Even today, our daughter likes to have a few friends over for homemade peach ice cream on her birthday. But city folk just don't properly know how to enjoy homemade ice cream. They will have one or two polite little bowls and then don't want anymore. That's definitely not the right farm boy way to eat homemade ice cream!

One sad night that stands out in our annals of ice cream eating occurred when we loaned out the ice cream churn to neighbors and the next time we made ice cream it was inedible. They hadn't washed out the ice cream container as well as they should have and we had to throw away two and a half gallons of ice cream. That dashed everybody's high expectations leaving us all a dejected bunch of Skupins.

Country Boy Cooking Tip: When making homemade ice cream, use lots of ice cream salt. When the ice cream begins to get stiff add fruit (maybe tree ripened peaches if they are available.) Once the ice cream is made, take out the dasher (eat a little ice cream) and then cover well and let sit for an hour to finish hardening. Eat a very light meal while waiting (a small sandwich.) Then eat ice cream until you can't see straight. It was impolite to eat less than four or five bowls full.

Skupin Homestead - Briary Texas

History Lesson #4.
Electricity Came Late to the Farm

Everyone realizes that life must have been very different back in historic time. But life on the farm in my childhood was so radically different from today it is hard for me to remember that I lived such a simple life only 60 years ago.

I want to begin by backing up to give a perspective about where we are today compared with what preceded us. I believe there were only a few automobiles of any kind in the entire state of Texas at the time my parents were born about 1907. Now I am not talking about my grandparents here, but about my parents. That is correct. 100 years ago there were almost no cars anywhere, and further, there was very little paved road either, in the entire state. Ford did not begin rolling Model Ts off the assembly line until late 1913.

Obviously, we all know from reading history books that very few cars or airplanes existed back then because they were just being invented. Nevertheless we seldom, if ever, stop and remember that our parents and grandparents lived in that time. I wonder how often they went to town if they had to ride eight miles in a buckboard pulled by a couple of mules? That is why little country stores, churches, and schools existed about every five miles sprinkled throughout rural areas. And after doing morning chores, the children walked to school barefoot in the snow, uphill both ways, every day. At least that is what we were told.

People were born, lived out their entire lives, died, and most of them never traveled more than 100 miles from home. Today, when we drive 15 miles on a freeway, we see thousands of cars and more concrete than existed in the whole state of Texas at the time my parents were born. My wife's father described driving from Laredo to San Antonio and having to stop and open cattle gates, drive through the gates, and then shut them so the cows wouldn't get out. Today the cattle gates are long gone and we call that road Interstate 35.

But there were exceptions, of course, and some people did travel far from where they were born. Dad's parents both left homes in Czechoslovakia and came to America, each separately and on their own in 1905, give or take a couple of years. They met in South Texas. Coming to the United States was a huge event in those days. Most of us have ancestors that came to America not many generations ago. When they took that trip they had to know they would probably never see home again. Many of them would also never see their parents, brothers or sisters, or any other relatives ever again.

The Wright Brother's didn't make their first flight at Kitty Hawk until 1903 and my mother was born four years later and Dad was born two years after that. What would the Wright Brothers think if they saw an airport like Bush International in Houston today? I suspect very few buildings would have had an elevator back then so even a "skyscraper" wouldn't have been over six or seven stories tall.

The first interstate freeways in the entire USA weren't built until the mid 1950's and that meant that almost no overpasses existed before then. Most highways in 1950 were still one lane each way. Those roads are called two lane roads, of course, and if you wanted to go faster than the car in front of you, then you had wait for a break in the oncoming traffic so you could pass. Have you noticed that many young city folk drive way over the speed limit on freeways but are uncomfortable passing cars on two lane roads today? That is because they have had little experience passing other cars in that situation and learning to judge the distance needed to pass safely takes a lot of practice.

I was born in 1942, which is even more recent. I was born at home, not in a hospital, and our home didn't have running water, which means it did not have indoor toilets. Let your mind run and imagine a world like the one I was born into. On a farm in central Texas there were no refrigerators, no hot water heaters, no air conditioning, and only wood or coal burning stoves for cooking and heating. For lights my parents used kerosene lanterns. I know Mom kept my older brother Robert's milk, in a bucket that was tied to a rope and lowered into the well to keep it cool. Obviously, there wouldn't be anything with a computer chip for another 40 years. The list is endless.

What about electricity? No farms had electricity until the REA (Rural Electrification Association) was created during the early days of Franklin Roosevelt's Presidency, which began in 1932. Belfalls Electric Coop was established in Rosebud, Texas in November of 1937 and it would have taken at least five years from that time to provide widespread electrical coverage to the surrounding rural area. That is correct. Almost no one living on a farm in central Texas had electricity until just two or three years before I was born.

Aunt Jodie says there were places around Clarkson that did not get electricity until the 1950's. Funny that Aunt Jodie would remember that. I suspect that her living in the Clarkson area had something to do with her sharp recall. Not only that, there were extremely few battery operated devices. Of course that not only meant no TVs, but also not even any radios. Just think—if you are old enough to read this—you have been around a lot longer than electricity had been on any farm in central Texas at the time I was born.

We had an old Ford pickup with a single bench seat when I was little. I remember going to town with Dad one Saturday afternoon in late 1948 and coming home with our first car, a brand new black 1949 Ford. Knowing Dad, I'm sure he wrote a check to pay for the car. He did not believe in using credit and only bought something when he could pay for it in full. No one had a credit card because they had not been invented either.

When I was about eight, Dad had a big propane tank buried in the back yard behind the kitchen and then we had gas. A little after that, we got a gas kitchen cook stove and then gas heaters for the kitchen, living room, and bathroom. Mother did not have to cook on a wood stove anymore.

But we continued to use a wood burning stove in the living room if we were going to keep the room warm all day (like on a Sunday) because wood was free. There weren't any chain saws but we had a pasture that had all of the wood we could use as long as someone took an axe and chopped wood for the stove. Most days we didn't heat the living room at all. However, we might light the gas heater in the evening because Mother and Grandma quilted in there in the winter.

When we got up in the morning, in the middle of the winter, it was about as cold inside as it was outside. Dad would get up first and light the heaters in the bathroom and the kitchen. While Mom cooked breakfast, Dad would shave before going outside to milk the cows. When Dad came back in from milking he would get everyone else up and we would push and shove to get a spot where we could back up to the kitchen heater to warm our backside until our pants were hot. Another good thing about having propane heat for the kitchen stove is we could easily warm a pot of water to wash our hands and face. Yes, just because we had a gas kitchen stove did not mean we had a hot water heater. Not quite yet, anyway.

Now I can't even imagine having to build a fire in a wood stove and then heat enough water to take a bath every time we got dirty. Farmers get dirty every day, especially in the summer time. Wood stoves had water tanks built into them so if the stove was fired up, you had a couple of gallons of hot water. Still, I suspect we took a lot of spit baths and a lot of the baths we took in the summer time were in cold water. It was a different time.

Mom's Country Wisdom: There's a cloud in the East. It's not going to rain.

Country Boy Manners: Don't dunk your bread in the gravy. It is bad manners. (Oh well, nobody's perfect.)

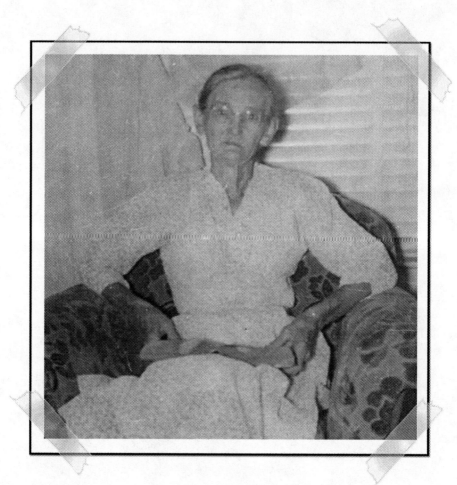

Grandma Engbrock

History Lesson #5.
Grandma Lived with Us

Grandma Mary Engbrock lived with us as far back as I can remember. Grandfather Robert Engbrock died when I was one year old. I don't know if this is correct but I seem to remember being held in someone's arms looking down in the casket at my grandfather and someone saying, "Isn't it a shame he will never know his grandfather." Family lore says that it was all of the grain dust that killed him but of course I don't know. I do know that he was often the fiddler when they had square dancing on Saturday night at the local country school, which also served as a community center. I also remember stories about him brewing his own beer and having the bottles pop open from the heat in the summer time.

After Grandfather Engbrock died, Grandma lived in her home near Pond Creek for a while. Then for several years she alternated between staying with us and with Aunt Clara, her other daughter. Eventually, probably when I was about 5, she just stayed with us. Grandma worked very hard and was an important part of the family. She helped cook, wash clothes, and clean. But she also worked outside a lot, doing hard physical work like chopping weeds, picking cotton, and working in the garden, as well as preparing, canning, and freezing food.

As part of their household chores, Mom and/or Grandma made 3 loaves of homemade bread twice a week. The day they made the homemade bread we would probably eat about a half of a loaf of warm freshly baked bread like kids eat potato chips today. You know. Bet you can't eat just one slice (with butter and Mom's fig preserves.) After we got home from school each day, Grandma would cut us each a couple of pieces of homemade bread and fry it in homemade butter and add a little cinnamon. Umm Boy! That was the good life. Grandma always took good care of us kids. Fresh homemade bread is hard to beat and the smell of bread baking is sure to bring back a few good memories from a time long past. Not bad pickings as I recall.

She liked to crochet at night after we all went to bed. Three of her bigger crochet projects were a tablecloth for the dining room table, a bedspread for her bed and a four-foot by six-foot picture of the Lord's Last Supper. I can almost hear her wailing when she discovered she had missed a crochet stitch and had to take out a big piece and do it over. Mom and Grandma also made quilts together every winter. They just didn't know how to not stay busy.

A few years after Grandma passed away Mom told us that she used to buy snuff for her at Aunt Clara's store. Apparently she liked to put a little tobacco under her lip while she crocheted late at night. We boys never had a clue.

Grandma also picked cotton every year and helped scrap cotton and corn. What does scrap cotton or scrap corn mean? (Historically this was called gleaning.) When you gather a crop there is always some left in the field. For instance, some cotton boles open after the harvest is over. Also some corn stalks fall down and the corn picker can't pick them up in order to gather their ears of corn, and other corn stalks at the end of the row get knocked down as the corn picker turns to get lined up on the next row.

Scrapping is going out and gathering what would otherwise be plowed under and lost. Dad gave us 100% of everything we got scrapping. It was pretty slow work but if you got the full value of what you gathered it was good money, and sources for earning money were scarce for Grandma. The heat was intense in August but Grandma never let that keep her from working come picking and scrapping time. We only worked where there was enough scrapping to make it worthwhile because our time to finish was limited. Farmers plowed cotton under a few weeks after the harvest to help control boll weevils and bollworms.

While living with us Grandma would raise about 50 turkeys each year and sell them before Thanksgiving to earn a little money. Turkeys are really dumb. Dumber than dumb. I am told that when it is raining a turkey might look up, open its mouth, and drown from the falling rain. I never saw that happen, but I have seen turkeys fight a snake. They form a circle around the snake and attack the tail of the snake until they kill it. Pretty smart huh? Well it is as long as you have enough turkeys to make a big circle. If the circle is too small the snake can start winning because he can get close enough to attack on his head end.

Some nights we couldn't find the turkeys to bring them home and pen them up. Wild dogs might find them and attack. The turkeys would panic and before you knew it you had a pile of dead turkeys.

One day one of Grandma's turkeys flew up on top of our new Ford car and Robert went to chase it off. Apparently the turkey was happy with its perch on the car and did not jump down when Robert ran out waving a baseball bat at it. Unfortunately, Robert got a bit aggressive and hit the turkey with the bat and the turkey died from the injuries. Grandma was madder than a wet hen and she let him know it. It took a little longer than usual for the "turkey incident" to be dropped from things discussed at the kitchen table.

In her later life Grandma received an old age pension from the state of Texas. It wasn't a lot of money but it was a whole lot more than nothing. Social Security is kind of like an old age pension was back then but she didn't pay into a separate tax to draw her pension.

Our two-bedroom house was too small when Grandma came to live with us, so my parents had a breezeway and a small one-car garage added onto the house. The breezeway functioned as a third bedroom. Both sides of the breezeway were end-to-end screen windows with heavy aluminum shutters installed over the screen windows.

The breezeway had a concrete floor and a double bed. Robert and I slept out there. It was a great place to sleep on a hot summer night but wintertime was a different story. The metal shutters leaked air like a sieve, so believe me it was more than a wee bit chilly out there on a frosty winter night. We had a feather bed, which was about the size of a mattress, but was filled with feathers. I liked to sleep on top of the feather bed so it would fluff up around me and keep the cold air from seeping in—especially under three or four of Mom's quilts.

Sleeping in the breezeway in the middle of the winter took fortitude. Every night I dreaded crawling between those ice-cold sheets. It was tempting to curl up in a cozy little ball when I first got into bed. That would quickly create a warm spot, but then, if I was going to stretch out before I went to sleep, I would have to suffer the pain of the cold sheets all over again when I slid my legs beyond the bounds of that warm spot.

So I would stretch out fully as soon as I got into the bed. Sure, it was cold, cold, cold, all over but it was kind of like jumping into a cold swimming pool rather than trying to ease into it a few inches at a time. It seemed to me as if that created a nice long warm cozy nest as quickly as possible.

When I was 10, Mom and Dad decided we had to add an actual third bedroom so David wouldn't have to sleep with Grandma anymore. Dad hired the best carpenter in town and, along with one of the farm hands, helped the carpenter build that bedroom and a small porch with a wash basin on the back of the house so we could wash our hands and face before going inside.

The new bedroom was large enough for two double beds. It was attached to the house on one side and there were windows on the other three sides of the room—eight windows in all. The new bedroom was not as cold and drafty in the winter as the breezeway yet when we opened the windows in the summertime, we still had great air circulation. To make it even better, Robert went away to college a couple of years later and David and I each had our own bed.

Grandma got skin cancer on the top of her head when I was 8 years old, say in 1950. Dr. Sweptson said there was nothing he could do, but a new hospital called M D Anderson had been opened in Houston and they might be able to help her. We all drove down to Houston so she could be treated.

M D Anderson made a big impression on me because there were patients without noses, without ears, you name it. I don't think it had been opened for patients very long and the treatment was research and therefore free. They cut a circle of cancerous skin off the top of Grandma's head about 4 inches across and grafted skin there from her thigh. She wore her hair in a bun on the back of her head after that and never tried to conceal that big bald spot.

We returned to M D Anderson twice a year for her checkups. Since treating cancer was new technology they followed up regularly to see if the treatment was indeed working. To get there we drove into Houston on the Hempstead highway and to downtown via Washington Ave. Then we took South Main Street to the medical center. It seemed like there was a stop light on every corner.

Someone suggested to my dad that he might be able to get home more quickly if he took Bellaire way, way out west of town and then looped back to the Hempstead highway on a two-lane road called South Post Oak. That was so far out of town that there was nothing out there but tall pine trees. It was almost scary driving through the forest late in the afternoon on that strange empty road. Of course, South Post Oak later became Houston's West Loop and today it is an extremely congested freeway nowhere near the edge of town. The Galleria is just outside of the West Loop and those pine trees are only a distant memory.

When I was 17 and in high school Grandma got lung cancer. It was too advanced to treat and she was sent home to die in her own bed. It was hard to lie in bed in the next room and listen to her pain as she gasped for every breath the last few weeks before her death.

Like Mom and Dad, she didn't hug or kiss us much. That was typical of the times, but there was no doubt in our minds that she loved us and she was as good a grandmother as I could possibly ask for. My brothers and I loved her dearly and she was an invaluable part of our lives.

> Grandma's Way of Cooking: When making a fruit pie, use a lot of fresh fruit. Sprinkle a little flour, sugar, and cinnamon between the layers of fruit. Add some dabs of butter between layers, too. Stack the fruit on deep. And don't add any of that store bought syrupy pie filling. Try it. It will make the best pie you have ever put in your mouth.

Robert on Sally

History Lesson #6.
One-Room School

We didn't have preschool or kindergarten in rural areas in those days, so both my brother Robert and I started school in the first grade in the one-room schoolhouse at Briary. My 1st grade year the entire school had 13 kids, one teacher (Mrs. Barnes) and she taught all three grades. Mrs. Barnes alternated teaching 1st grade arithmetic one year and second grade arithmetic the next year. She was teaching 2nd grade arithmetic when I was in the 1st grade. But she must have done a good job because when I went to college I got a degree in Math.

Mrs. Barnes would fill a bucket with rain water, which had run off of the roof and down a gutter into the cistern, each morning. The bucket was brought inside and when we wanted a drink we all drank from the same dipper. At least we never had to worry about the other kids putting their mouth on the water fountain.

But think about it. No running water meant no indoor toilets. The restrooms were out behind the school, where the boys had a three holer and I assume the girls' restroom was also a three holer. A three holer is an outhouse with three seats. There was a deep hole in the ground under each seat, of course, but once again—no running water. I can't really say they smelled wonderful, but you got used to it and they weren't quite as bad as you might think. The outhouse was not a place to meet and greet your friends as school restrooms are today.

That school was a little less than two miles from our house. Someone always took me to school but if the weather was decent I usually walked home. Donald Wayne, a 1st grade classmate, would walk about 1/3rd of the way with me but I had to walk the rest of the way by myself.

On the last day of school before Christmas of my 1st grade year, I was walking home by myself. When I got half way home my right side was hurting terribly. It hurt so bad I just wanted to sit down and cry but I knew I needed to keep walking to get to Mom. So I kept putting one foot in front of the other despite the pain. When I finally got home Mom and Dad took one look at me, felt my forehead, and rushed me into town to see Dr. Sweptson. I had an emergency appendectomy late that afternoon.

However, I could never do anything the simple way. While recuperating from surgery I developed a severe case of pneumonia and was extremely sick over the entire Christmas holidays. I still remember a tube that ran into a 5-gallon jug that ended up almost half full of fluids that had drained from my lungs.

I did learn to play checkers while in the hospital and I guess I was a quick learner because it seemed as if I won almost every game. Usually I played Mom or a cousin. I was there nearly two weeks and I was almost never left alone. It was the custom that a relative or close friend stayed at the hospital with a patient in those days.

Even when my dad had surgery almost 20 years later, I took vacation and went home so either Mom or I could stay with him day and night. When someone was in the hospital friends would come to visit even if they didn't stay very long. I may have been sick as a dog, but I had lots of relatives and family friends come visit. That was common courtesy and one doesn't mess with common courtesy. Right? Right!

But before I go on, I want to tell a story about my older brother Robert when he attended that one room school. One day Dad and a neighbor (Nollie Henson only lived about four miles away which made him a neighbor in our part of the world) went to a livestock auction barn in Temple and Mr. Henson bought a pony for his son Charles. Mr. Henson did not have a cattle trailer with him so he asked Dad if he could take the pony home and keep him in our in our pasture until Christmas, which was just a few days away. When he came to get the pony he looked down at Robert, who had tears in his eyes because he had learned to love the pony in those few days. Anyway, Dad bought the pony from Mr. Hensen and we named her Sally.

Robert rode Sally to school each day. The teacherage (the house provided by the school district for the teacher to live in), which was next to the school, had a barn where Robert kept Sally until school was out, and then he rode her home. Dad noticed that Robert, who was probably only in the 3rd grade, was walking Sally to school and he told Robert that he could kick her a little and get her to walk a little faster or even trot. Dad said he looked up the next day and Robert had Sally at a full gallop with her tail straight out as he rode her to school.

You probably noticed in the picture preceding this chapter that Robert is riding Sally bareback. That is because we did not own a saddle until about the time I got into high school. Sally did have a few tricks. Once we got a saddle, Sally would fill her belly with air, like many horses do when you tightened the girth, and then let it out after you thought you had it tight. Loose saddle right? That is correct. So it was back to tightening the girth a little more.

Sally had three knots on her stomach immediately behind her left front leg that we never noticed until we got a saddle. The girth rubbed those three knots and they would become open sores if we used a saddle every day. I suspect those knots may have had something to do with why the previous owner sold her to Mr. Hensen.

I once rode Sally four miles to Aunt Clara's store and then rode her back home. But it wasn't like in the movies. I let her walk most of the way. If you got her into a trot she would jar every bone in your body, and she knew what she was doing, too. So it was walk or gallop and you can't run a horse for very long unless you train it to have endurance.

About half way to the store I had to cross a wooden bridge. It is not unusual for horses to shy away from things that people take for granted. She could see light between those wood planks and would not go across the bridge until I got off and led her across. It took most of a half day but we did get to the store and back home. I felt good about making that long journey on Sally, however, it really wasn't very much fun, so I never did that again.

Another time I rode Sally about 2 1/2 miles to see my friend John Allen. He also had a horse so we could play "Cowboys and Indians" in the woods in their pasture. I learned real quickly that riding at a gallop in a pasture near trees is not as romantic as it looks in the movies. The horse always seems to go under the low hanging branches. Even a tiny branch hurts like the dickens when you are riding a horse at full gallop and it hits you in the face. Just about the time the sting goes away enough to open your eyes again, another branch creates a few additional tears.

That covers most of my stories about Sally; so back to school we go. At the end of my first grade year the one room school in Briary was closed and the entire Briary area was consolidated into the Rosebud School District. Our house was four highline poles (electric power line poles) from the public road, where we caught the school bus at our mailbox. I kicked many a rock while I walked that lane to catch the bus or while walking home after the bus dropped us off. I would also ride my bicycle past those four highline poles to get the mail.

Sometimes while we were only half way from our house to the bus stop we would see the school bus come into view about a half-mile away. Since we could see the bus coming we would run like crazy to catch it. Of course Mr. Lierman would wait on us if we didn't quite make it but no one would lollygag and make the bus wait on them if they were not at the bus stop when the bus got there.

Everyone, 1st grade through 12th grade, rode the same bus. We caught the bus about 7:20 in the morning as it was headed away from Rosebud and we completed the bus route and were in school by 8:00 when the bell rang. I think the school day ended at 4:00 o'clock. Elementary school kids had a play period at the end of the school day while they waited for the high school kids to be dismissed.

Two popular playground games back in elementary school were marbles and tops. Depending on the season every boy would go to school each morning with either a pocket full of marbles or a pocket full of tops. Marbles was played by drawing a circle in the dirt and each participant placing a marble in the circle. We took turns, each trying to capture the other peoples' marbles by knocking them out of the circle with our favorite shooter marble, which we shot with our thumb.

Playing marbles "for keeps" (which meant if you captured the other person's marble you got to keep it) was strictly forbidden, so we only played for keeps as long as a teacher did not come along and observe. Teachers usually kept their distance and were careful not to watch too closely. Tops was similar to marbles but the stakes were higher since a top cost more than a marble. While the boys were shooting marbles or throwing tops the girls were frequently jumping rope or playing jacks.

Riding a bus for over an hour a day is an experience in itself. I tried to sit next to my friends, and I can't remember what we talked about, but we talked non-stop. If the seats next to your better friends were already taken, you had to take whatever was available. We did not sit next to the same person every day.

In general the older kids sat towards the back of the bus and the younger ones sat up closer to the driver. Getting stuck next to one of the pretty White twins who were Robert's age wasn't all that bad either. Even though we lived scattered through the country we did get to talk for almost two hours each day on the bus.

Patricia Wimberly was in the grade below me and lived across the road from the far side of our farm. It was a pretty good distance by public road so we hardly ever played together. However, she was one of the few girls my age that I ever played with. I didn't spend much time talking to girls on the bus but I must have talked to her some.

Patricia wore her hair in pigtails in elementary school and that was just more temptation than the average boy could take. If you sat behind her on the bus or in school, you just had to reach up and give one of those pigtails a tug. It wasn't fair; you had no choice. But once you pulled it, Patricia made you wish you hadn't.

Patricia tried out to be a cheerleader her first year in high school. I doubt if anyone thought that she had a chance because freshmen just didn't get elected cheerleader. The candidates tried out in pairs and they would get on the stage and do a polite cheer together. But when Patricia's turn came she hollered her cheer as loud as if she were leading the crowd at a game and of course she was elected cheerleader by the student body all four years. It was a great example to me of what one can accomplish if they don't let their inhibitions get in the way.

Looking back on how frugal my parents were I find it a bit surprising that we didn't take our lunch to school, but every Monday morning Mother gave us lunch money for the whole week. Lunches were 25 cents until we got to high school and 35 cents after that. The mothers of my classmates, Jackie McCollum and Mary Lou Lierman, both worked in the cafeteria and in general the food was pretty good.

Cream corn was the one clear exception. I never liked it anyway but one day in high school I decided to give it a chance and then promptly threw it up. That confirmed in my mind that creamed corn was indeed awful and I was never tempted to eat another bite of it again.

Obviously there was quite a bit of racial discrimination in those days. The black kids not only went to a different school, they even had a separate bus. The Mexican kids went to my school but they sat on the back two rows of the school bus. Otherwise they played sports and participated in many of the other school activities. Nevertheless, I am sure they felt like they were not fully included in school life. Discrimination was a fact of life and unfortunately still is, even though it has improved quite a lot through the years.

In the fifth grade I had Mr. Davis for a teacher. He was also the elementary school principal. Amazingly enough, Mr. Davis had also taught my Dad and Robert. But when my younger brother reached the 5th grade Mr. Davis taught the other section so David never had him for a teacher. Mr. Davis was the first male teacher I ever had. I thought all of my elementary school teachers were wonderful even if Mr. Davis was just a bit stern.

Dad said that when he was in school the boys would go down to the outhouse and smoke and Mr. Davis would see the smoke and come racing down there to try and catch them. But they had a bunch of unique ways of putting out the cigarettes quickly and hiding them from him. No, my dad never really took up smoking. Except for Grandpa Skupin, who smoked a pipe, the only relative I had that ever smoked was Aunt Clara's husband, Uncle Jim. And lung cancer took him fairly young.

Sometimes I would have boys from my class come out to the farm and spend Friday night with me. One Saturday John Tarver and I caught Sally so we could ride her. I rode a little and then John got on to ride. Sally turned around and went under the clothesline. Before you could say "Jack Frost" the clothesline drug John off Sally and he landed on his backside. We will never know, of course, but it sure seemed like Sally went under that clothesline on purpose. John was ok after a few minutes, but we may have put Sally back in the pasture after the clothesline adventure.

In the 6th grade I started playing football. The junior high team dressing room was affectionately known as the "Rat Hole." That probably gives it more credit than it deserves. It was in the basement of the high school building and I believe it was originally used to store coal. It had no windows and little ventilation. All we had were hooks for organizing our uniforms and clothes.

After walking about 10 feet down a narrow stairs to get into the dressing room we had to walk up another set of stairs to shower. I don't ever remember hot water in the Rat Hole shower. Since the shower was elevated about 6 feet above the dressing room, showering was kind of like being naked on a raised stage. I am sure most of us suffered irreparable psychological damage from showering in the Rat Hole. I would cringe when the cold water hit me and the other boys would laugh at me but I have always hated an ice cold shower. The only positive thing I can say about the Rat Hole is that it makes a good war story today.

Rosebud was a small school and I remember about 45 students in my class in the 6th grade. But "the times they were a changing" and it took fewer and fewer people to work the land, so the farm population was declining rapidly. Businesses were closing and people were moving to Dallas, Waco, and Houston. Also cars and roads had improved enough that locals were driving further to shop in Cameron and Temple. We must have had a fairly large dropout rate also. Even with a few added students when small schools like Westphalia, Travis, and Burlington all consolidated into our school in Rosebud, we only had 33 students left in our entire class by the time I graduated.

Just a few years later the Rosebud Black Panthers, with school colors of black and gold, and the Lott Lions, with school colors of black and white, consolidated school districts and became the Rosebud-Lott Cougars with school colors of black, gold, and white.

I don't recall the exact timeline, but integration occurred about the same time as the consolidation of the Rosebud-Lott schools. The Rosebud black school was closed and integrated into the new Rosebud-Lott consolidated school district. A new high school was built half way between Rosebud and Lott in Travis (opening in January 1972) and old Rosebud high schools was torn down. I suppose there was a black school in Lott also but I don't remember any other details about the integration and consolidation because I was no longer living in the area.

> Schoolyard Country Wisdom: If the sun was shining at the same time it was raining, the kids would say the devil was beating his wife.

David in Backyard
Smoke House in Background

History Lesson #7.
Like a Chicken with Its Head Chopped Off

Most of us eat beef, pork, poultry, and fish which we buy in the grocery store and never think much about where it comes from or how it got there. But when you raise animals on the farm for the purpose of selling them to be eaten, killing animals is just a fact of life. You must kill an animal before you can butcher it, cook it, and eat it.

When you grow up seeing your parents do it, then that is just the way things are done. But it does teach you to be a little careful about being too attached to some of the farm animals. Dogs, cats, and horses were pets, but cows, calves, chickens, pigs, and turkeys were never serious pets because sooner or later they were going to be eaten or sold.

I don't remember the exact month, but sometime in the middle of the winter each year we went to the hatchery in Cameron and bought about 75 tiny yellow chicks. They would only be a few days old and they were so cute we would just sit and watch them running around in and out from under the brooder cheeping away and pecking for food.

For the first few months of their lives they lived in the separate building we called a brooder house. Inside this nursery for the baby chicks there was a sort of incubator (called a brooder) which was a tin pyramid about 18 inches high and four feet wide with a couple of big light bulbs inside to create warmth. The brooder sat a few inches off the floor so the tiny chicks could walk in under the edge (when they got cold) and back out (when it got too warm or they wanted to explore). The little chicks would huddle close together under the brooder to keep warm on a cold night.

Young chickens grow up to be fryers by late spring and the time would come to begin turning those young chickens into food for our table. In order to do that Mom, Grandma, and one or two of us boys would all pitch in and work together to process about 15 fryers in a day.

Mom froze about 55 fryers each spring that we would eat year around. There were several different ways to kill a chicken. First we had to catch them with a chicken hook. A chicken hook was about a 4-foot piece of stiff wire about the thickness of a pencil. The last three inches were bent back to form a hook a little less than half an inch across. If you hooked that end around a chicken's leg, the chicken would be caught.

After you caught the chicken you had to kill it. I think most people grabbed the chicken by the head and spun it to break the chicken's neck, but Mother did not like to do that. It was just a little too vicious for her. Also she might have been afraid she would only injure the chicken and not kill it. Instead, she drove two large nails about an inch apart into a log. She would place the chicken's neck between the two nails and since the chicken's head was wider than the two nails, the chicken's neck could be pulled taunt. Mom then took a hatchet and chopped the chicken's head off. It wasn't very pretty but it was efficient. The chicken died every time as far as I can remember.

Once the head had been chopped off she quickly threw the chicken a few feet away so she wouldn't get blood splattered all over herself when the chicken flopped around as it bled to death. Have you ever heard the expression "running around like a chicken with its head chopped off?" Well it comes from the fact that they do run and flop around after their heads are cut off. That's kind of creepy but it was just a fact of life for us farm kids.

Before we caught the first chicken, Mom would have started a fire under that big black kettle in the back yard to boil a pot full of water. She would dip out a bucket full, hold the dead chicken by the legs and dunk it into the boiling water several times to get the feathers soaked to the skin. This made it possible, though not particularly easy, to pull out the chicken's feathers. Pulling out the feathers is called plucking the chicken and it probably takes about 15 minutes of hard work to pluck one chicken.

But we had a good workforce and as the old saying goes "many hands make light work."

Robert might be helping Dad on the farm (or he may have already left home). Once we plucked all of the big feathers, the "down" (the furry little feathers that were underneath the large outer feathers) would stick to our hands making it hard to see where we had finished and where we needed to get the last few feathers in order to do a good job.

Mom singed the remaining down that we did not quite get off by holding the chicken over a fire and turning it slowly, kind of like you roast a marshmallow. If you singed the feathers in the kitchen the burning odor permeated ever corner of the house and lingered for hours so this was usually done outside.

Then the chicken had to be cleaned. That means the chicken must be cut open and the intestines, heart, lungs, and all of the other innards removed. A few of the organs, like the gizzard, heart, and liver, were washed, cooked, and eaten but the guts were thrown away. Mom would then cut up and pack the cleaned chicken in a freezer box or bag and freeze it to be eaten later. On a day she processed chickens, we would probably eat fried chicken for lunch or dinner.

If you look closely at the picture in front of this chapter of David in the back yard, you can see Mom coming out of the chicken house on the far left. You can also see Grandma, in silhouette, entering the kitchen through the back door of the house. The small open shed between the smokehouse and the chicken house was just a storage nook.

We did shut the door to the chicken house each night, once the chickens went in and got up on their roost, but that was to protect them from any wild animals. The chicken house was a fairly large room with a slanted roost the chicken could jump up on to sleep. The egg nests were hung from the ceiling where the chickens could hop up into them from near the top of the roost. The front wall faced south and was made of chicken wire, which allowed the winter sun to shine in and provided ventilation in the summer.

Another interesting building in the picture is the smokehouse, seen between the house and the henhouse. It was used as a workspace for Mom, as a place for the washing machine, to make lye soap, and for storage. And of course, if we slaughtered a hog we would actually use the smokehouse to smoke the sausage.

I definitely remember the really cool baseball glove David is using in the picture. It may have been Robert's originally but it probably wasn't very good even way back then. Without any doubt it would have been easier to catch a ball barehanded than with that glove, but real ball players all have to have a glove!

> Mom's Country Wisdom: I wouldn't be able to find my own head if it wasn't screwed on.

Little League Baseball

History Lesson #8.
Little League Baseball

When I was young, our barn was old and very close to our house. One day there was a tractor parked out by that old barn and I climbed up on it to play. I cocked the throttle back wide open, shifted the gears and turned on the key, things I had seen my Dad do, but I certainly didn't have a clue about what I was doing. I was just playing and I doubt if I was more than six. Anyway I pushed a button that turned out to be the starter and the engine roared to life at full throttle.

They told me you could hear me screaming in the next county and everybody came running—Mom, Dad, Grandma, and who knows who all else. Fortunately the last thing I had done before pushing the starter button, was to move the gear shift into neutral, so the engine roared but the tractor went nowhere. Since the tractor was facing the barn it would have been pretty disastrous if it had been in gear. I'm very glad I never found out what might have happened.

Shortly thereafter, Dad decided he needed a bigger barn and he wanted to build it a couple of hundred yards away from the house to get the stink of cow manure farther from our daily life. So a new barn was built and the old barn was torn down. That left a large yard beside our house that had been well fertilized by the accumulation of years of cow manure. We planted Bermuda grass on that big yard and the grass flourished.

The bad part of having a huge lawn was that someone had to mow it and I was often that someone. We didn't live in town so we probably only mowed it about every three weeks. If the grass got too long and the shredder happened to be hooked to a tractor, Dad or my older brother would just shred the field and that probably only took them about 15 minutes. A shredder is a lot like a giant lawn mower and today we often see them mowing the weeds along the sides of the highway in the summer time. Back then it would have been about 6 feet wide, though they are much wider today.

Robert helped me build a baseball backstop in the corner of the new lawn and I had a baseball field even if I seldom had anyone close to my age to play ball with. However, when I was in the 6th grade Mother threw me a birthday party and we invited all of the boys in my 6th grade class to come out to our farm for my celebration.

Mother cooked pinto beans, fried chicken, and a birthday cake, of course, and I'm sure there were potatoes and other good eats. She put bacon and maybe even a little bacon dripping in the beans and I loved them. We all used ketchup on beans to enhance the flavor, kind of like kids use ketchup on French fries today.

We played baseball all day long, only stopping long enough to eat the lunch Mother and Grandma had prepared. Anyway, our birthdays were recognized each year and we always had a cake but that was the only birthday party I ever had and it still gives me a warm feeling when I think about it.

In 1953 and 1954 I played Little League Baseball in the summer. Being allowed to play baseball was pretty unusual when you lived on the farm with all of the chores that needed doing. By the time school was out in May, the crops were planted and it was too early for harvesting. Anyway, I was still just a little too young for things like chopping cotton and I couldn't drive yet.

But there was one problem. Neither Dad nor Robert had time to take me to practice and Mom never drove to town or on paved roads because she did not have a driver's license. Basically, Mom only drove in the fields and the four miles of gravel road to her sister's country store, where she did most of our shopping.

Little League teams did not have rules restricting how much we practiced in those days so we practiced every morning five days a week and again that afternoon if we did not have a game that night. The Slovacek's lived about a quarter of a mile away through the field. They went to town each morning to work and I could catch a ride into town with them for the morning practice. But I had to hitchhike to get to the afternoon practice and to get home from both practices.

Of course everybody on the southeast side of town knew my parents and if someone came by, I would "thumb a ride" and almost everybody would stop and give me a ride. I don't know any 11 year olds that are allowed to thumb a ride today. Let me tell you, I rode with some pretty interesting people. I particularly remember riding with a man that obviously had very little money. His car was ancient, had no muffler, and only had a seat for the driver. I sat on a bale of hay.

Either my parents or Robert drove me to the games. That is correct. We got our driver's license at 14 in those days in Texas. When Robert drove me to a game he was not always there to pick me up right when the game ended. They would turn out the lights on the ballpark and everybody would go home, and I mean everybody. Even Coach Hoelscher.

But that was fine with us. That was what we wanted. I would be left alone on the corner under the streetlight waiting for Robert to come back from whatever fooling around a teenager with a car might be up to. We never told Mom and Dad that Robert sometimes was not there when the game ended because they would have lit into him. So it was our secret. Can you imagine an 11 year old being left standing on a corner under a street light at 9:00 PM today—and all of the adults just turning out the ballpark lights and going home! And no one thought anything about it.

> Country comment (When you are looking for something and someone points out you are standing next to what you are trying to find): If it had been a snake it would have bit you.

Henry, Robert and Dad
With Farmall H Tractor

History Lesson #9.
A Telephone, a TV and a Hot
Water Heater

I wonder which of these we got first? I would guess we got a hot water heater before we got the TV but we simply couldn't get a telephone until later. Isn't that amazing? When it comes to priorities hot water would seem to come well before a luxury like a TV.

I was probably in junior high before we got any of them. In order to take a warm bath before we had a hot water heater, Mom had to boil water on the stove in the kitchen, carry it to the bathtub and dump it in. We never had much water in the tub when we took a bath and I think more than one kid may have sometimes taken a bath in the same water. After years and years of that, it was an amazing luxury to have as much hot water as we wanted, whenever we wanted.

Remember, just like us, most people did not have a telephone. When someone came to visit us they didn't call before they came. They just "dropped by" and we did the same when we went to visit them. Of course company would usually visit on Saturday night or Sunday afternoon. The dogs would announce their arrival by barking like crazy and chasing their car when they got near our house. However, we would often spot them coming kicking up a cloud of dust when they turned off the public gravel road and into the lane that led to our house.

It wouldn't be obvious to people today, but it was so quiet out there in the country that you could hear a car on the gravel roads from over a quarter mile away if the wind was in the right direction and the windows in the house were open, which they usually were. There was no hum of air conditioners or the traffic noise that we take for granted in cities today. When we saw visitors coming, Mother would holler for everyone to pick up quickly, grabbing any clutter that might be in the living room or dining room, throwing it into a bedroom, and closing the door.

Dad had tried to get a telephone for many years but the phone company just didn't have enough lines out on our side of town to handle any more customers. Finally the phone company put in entirely new telephone poles with enough wires to provide service to everyone in Briary who wanted a phone, and at last we could get a telephone. It was a wooden box that hung on the wall and had a hand crank.

All phones in the country were on party lines with about eight families sharing the same line. Each household had a different ring; ours for instance, was two long rings followed by a short ring. When any one phone on the party line was in use, every other phone was locked out from placing or receiving a call.

It was bad manners to tie up the party line for 30 minutes or more as teens today frequently do. The only way to find out if the phone line was busy was to pick up the phone and listen. Of course, if you had an emergency you could ask whoever was on the phone to hang up so you could make a quick call. It is hard to image sharing your phone with 20 or more people!

If we wanted to call another person on our party line, say the person with a long ring followed by a short one, we gave the crank a full turn followed by a half turn. If we wanted to call someone that was not on our party line, we had to call the operator by turning the crank a couple of turns and then she would place the call.

One thing I do remember is that Dad got a kick out of listening in to other people's conversations on our party line. If anyone on the party line got a phone call, every phone on that line rang. If you heard a ring of maybe two short rings, for instance, you knew it was not for you but you also knew who it **was** for. So Dad would quietly pick it up and listen to the conversation while Mother would flutter around in the background trying to get him to hang up. It was a different time.

Once the new phone system was completely installed we got a stylish black rotary dial phone and our phone no longer rang when the call was not for us. Our number was Jupiter 3-2283, and when we were calling someone else in Rosebud we did not have to dial the JU. We no longer had to get the operator to place a call for us, but it was still a party line and if someone else was using the phone when we picked it up, we still had to wait until they got off the phone before we could make our call.

When the phone company put in new poles and lines they left the old broken down wires dangling from their dilapidated poles. Since the old lines were no longer useable, the phone company told the farmers they could have the wire if they wanted it. So one more little thing I got to do was roll up the old telephone wire for Dad to use elsewhere. I probably rolled more than a half-mile of abandoned wire. I don't think Dad knew exactly what he would use it for but it was free so why not get it?

Naturally Dad did find some uses for the telephone wire but the main thing he used it for was to make electric fences. An electric fence was a single bare wire (not a barbed wire) that was strung where you wanted a temporary fence. For instance, if you wanted to let the cows graze in the corn patch after you finished harvesting the corn you had to put up a temporary fence around the corn patch to keep the cows from grazing on the other crops.

The temporary fence posts were just steel angle iron stakes that were driven into the ground. The electric wire had to be attached to an insulator, which did not conduct electricity. The insulators were attached to the steel posts and held a single strand of wire a couple of feet above the ground. An auto battery would be attached to a box called a fencer and the fencer would send an electric shock from the battery through the wire every couple of seconds.

Cows and horses would have just walked over the plain wire without the electrical shock but once they touched that wire a few times they quickly learned to stay away from it. Usually cows like to stick their head through a fence and eat the grass on the other side. When you used an electric fence, however, they would not graze within a couple of feet of it.

I vividly remember helping Dad install an electric fence one day. Instead of using an old style 6-volt battery, he used one of the new fangled 12-volt car batteries in order to create a little bigger jolt. Once he got the fence all set up, he grabbed the wire to make sure the jolts of electricity were strong enough. He held it a few seconds and said he did not think it was working right. So I grabbed the wire and it just about knocked me down.

Dad grabbed it again, scratched his head, and said something was still wrong. Then he asked me to test it again which I did and it shocked me like I'd been kicked by a mule. I was not about to do that a third time. Then Dad looked down at his feet and said, "Oh, it must be these rubber sole shoes I have on." Nope, rubber doesn't conduct much electricity so he was getting only a very light tingle while I was getting kicked into the next county.

My parents almost never went out to dinner at a restaurant. If Dad got trapped away from home at mealtime he might buy himself a hamburger for lunch, but I don't think I ever remember them dining out for the evening meal, not even once. They spent very little money on entertainment. They might go see a blockbuster movie like the "Ten Commandments" once a year, but they just didn't get out much. We did have a few close friends and family members who would come to see us occasionally and we would go to visit once in a while.

About 1954 Dad decided to get a fancy new 16-inch black and white Motorola TV. It was huge! No, the screen wasn't huge, just the "piece of furniture" that housed the TV. But there was one tiny little problem—there were no TV stations. Sure there was the brand new KCEN Temple TV station but it was probably 40 miles away. The next closest was Austin which was close to 100 miles, but their signal and the signal from the station in Dallas just did not come in very well at all. Channel 2, KPRC in Houston, had the second best reception and it was probably over 130 miles away as the crow flies.

So when Dad bought the TV he also bought a forty foot TV antenna with a motor on top. You could pivot the antenna 360 degrees while standing in front of the TV. One thing that made getting good reception difficult was that when you were standing next to the TV trying to adjust the picture (or the outside antenna) your body became a small antenna itself. Once you finally got a picture that you could just barely make out you would lose it as soon as you walked away from the TV. Today it is hard to remember how lousy the TV reception was back then, especially for rural people like us who lived so far from the nearest TV station.

Of course there wasn't any such thing as a remote control so you had to walk up to the TV to change channels, adjust the volume, and fine-tune the picture. On most days we only picked up one channel, therefore, we did not spend a lot of time changing channels.

I think we had the first TV in that part of the country. Well, I'm sure there were some in town but I really didn't know of anyone else out on our side of town with a TV yet. Never mind that the picture and sound was bad. We could just about make out when the people on the screen were moving and that was good enough. Once we got the TV, we did get a little more company than before, because our neighbors came over to gape at the novel sight.

Back in those days no one had many electrical gadgets. When I started working after college I had a car, I shared a two-bedroom apartment with a friend, we had a rotary dial telephone and my roommate had a black and white TV. About a year later I bought a stereo record player with an am/fm radio—from a door-to-door salesman.

When I got married my parents got a new color TV and gave us that old 16 inch black and white Motorola TV. It wasn't easy getting it from Rosebud to Houston. It was so big it would not fit in the car so we put it in the trunk. It was way too big to shut the trunk so we left it sticking out and tied the trunk lid down with a rope. It dominated the living room in our small apartment. We had none of the electrical stuff that young people must have today. Very few of those gadgets existed.

People who lived in the country in those days seldom locked their cars or their houses. Generally we would just leave our keys in the ignition of cars, trucks, and tractors. That way we never needed to go looking for a key when we wanted to use them. When I was young Dad even left the keys in the car in town. Taking the key out of the ignition when he got out of the car never became automatic for him.

Locking the house was even more unusual. Mother would put the hook on the screen door when we went to bed at night but I'm not sure why. As everyone knows, a screen door wouldn't even keep out an honest thief, if there were such a thing. We did have a pretty effective alarm system, provided by the barking dogs, even if the sheriff's department wasn't wired to come out and check every time they started raising a ruckus.

Country Boy Observation: I don't think most people are even aware that everything we buy is at least a couple of percent higher than back in my childhood just because we might pay for it with a credit card. And we accept those higher prices without realizing how credit cards have raised the cost of living, even if we pay cash.

Clara and Hattie Engbrock

History Lesson #10.
Aunt Clara's Store

Aunt Clara and Uncle Jim Hauk had a country store about four miles from us via the gravel road. Like I said, Mother did not have a driver's license and one of the few places she would drive was to her sister's store. Uncle Jim was also a farmer so Aunt Clara mostly ran the store by herself. I would never name drop, of course, but I find it interesting that Drayton McLane Sr. was the wholesaler who delivered to their store.

Well, I guess I might as well point out what everyone already knows, that Drayton McLane, Jr., the current owner of the Houston Astros, is huge in both trucking and wholesaling. I met Drayton Jr. at Aunt Clara's store a couple of times when he was in high school working as a helper on one of his father's wholesale trucks. Dad admired and kept up with Drayton McLane, Sr.'s business practices when very few people had ever heard of him, but that is a whole other story, that I won't go into here.

Aunt Clara's store was large for a country store and unique as far as I am concerned. There were two hand cranked Phillip 66 gas pumps in front of the store. The inside was about 50% bigger than most large convenience stores of today, not counting a storeroom and their living quarters. We bought almost everything there. In the summer Aunt Clara asked Mom (and her other regular customers) how many and what size blue jeans we would all need for the school year and she would order Wrangler jeans for us. I still wear Wranglers. At picking time she would have cotton sacks for cotton pickers to buy.

There was a meat counter where Mother would buy bacon custom sliced the thickness she wanted. (We didn't butcher a hog all that often so we usually had to buy bacon.) There was always baloney and summer sausage. She also carried a big round of Rat Cheese that was covered with a red wax rind and was just left out on the counter. You told her how much cheese you wanted and she would cut off a piece that size and weigh it to determine the price.

Aunt Clara would buy Mom's farm-raised eggs that we didn't eat and resell them to other customers. She would candle each egg to make sure it was edible. This involved placing the egg up against a hole in a stovepipe (not a heated stove pipe—this was a separate homemade device for candling eggs only.) The hole was not quite big enough for the egg to fit through. There was a strong light in the pipe. If she saw a dark spot inside the egg she knew it was fertile and an embryo had begun to develop so it was not usable.

The store had a multi drawer spool box with just about every color thread you could imagine. They also carried cigarettes, coal oil and a big bin with different size bolts and nails right out in the middle of the store. Aunt Clara had fresh vegetables, and a wide variety of food but a rather limited number of options for each type of food. For instance, there were about six choices for breakfast cereal. She always had Wheaties, Post Toasties, and Cheerios, and she rotated a few other varieties. Sometimes she might have Kix, Sugar Crisps and maybe Grape Nuts, for example (with only one size box of each type of cereal).

Aunt Clara also had onion plants, seeds for the garden, potato slips, Spam, sardines, and many other things. Since people had to do a lot of baking, most people bought flour in 25 or 50 pound sacks. Mom used the empty flour sacks for dishtowels. Mother always bought Gladiola flour because Grandma's brother, Len Bigler, advertised it every weekday at noon on WBAP in Dallas. He had a really golden radio voice and we all loved to hear his short radio ads each day. Our kitchen had a tapered (narrow at the bottom) flour bin that Mother would empty the sack of flour into. She would dip the flour sifter into that bin and get the flour she wanted in one quick movement. There is another term that adults know but kids seldom hear today, a flour sifter.

Chicken feed came in sacks made from attractive printed material. Mother (and the other women) would carefully select which sacks they wanted because they would make clothing (and quilts) from the fabric when the sacks were empty.

It is hard to imagine today but back then a candy bar, ice cream bar, or soft drink (we called it soda water) all cost a nickel and since I was a nephew I was allowed to select a nickel treat of my choice every time we went to the store. But I was not to ask for one. I was to wait until Aunt Clara offered it to me.

Soda water only came in bottles and the drink of choice for school kids was RC Cola. Other soft drinks kids liked were Nehi and Big Red. RC, Nehi, and Big Red all came in a twelve-ounce bottle and a Coke bottle was only six ounces. I'm pretty sure Coke had quite a bit of a sharper bite to it back then than a Coke has today. You were charged a deposit of two cents a bottle when you took bottles home but they gave you back the two cents when you returned the bottle. The used bottles were sent back to the bottler where they were washed and reused. Except for when I got a soda water at Aunt Clara's store, I very seldom had a soft drink.

Twist off caps on bottles had not been invented, so anyone wanting to open a beverage bottle had to use a bottle opener. The other end of the bottle opener could be used to punch a hole in a canned drink. Since one of the main drinks canned or bottled was beer, the opener was referred to factiously by many folk as a church key. Every house had several church keys and the dash of most cars also had one.

Back then it was common for people to drink a beer while riding around with their friends. Yes, that included the driver. Later, they began making cans from aluminum, which came with a pull-tab, so a church key was no longer required. However, carelessly discarded pull-tabs became an environmental problem, so the aluminum can manufactures invented a push to open tab. The push-tabs resulted in a lot of cut thumbs, so the current flip-up ring on cans replaced it.

Even today, I love it when a friend or relative does something that I consider entrepreneurial. Back when I was young, Uncle Jim decided to grow the newly developed technology of hybrid (cross-pollinated) corn and market it in their country store under his name. He solicited several farmers to help him grow the seed corn and Dad was one of the farmers that took part in this effort.

First, Uncle Jim selected two varieties of corn to crossbreed into his hybrid corn. Dad would plant two rows of Variety A seed that would be used to "cross-pollinate" the following six rows of Variety B. He would plant the entire corn patch repeating this pattern of two rows of Variety A followed by six rows of Variety B.

When the corn stalks reached full height and began to tassel out, Dad hired people to cut the tassels off the top of each stalk of the Variety B corn. This would only leave the tassels on the top of Variety A corn stalks to pollinate the whole field. (As you probably know, each kernel in an ear of corn must be pollinated by pollen from a tassel on the top of a corn stalk. The pollen from the tassel falls on the corn silks growing from the end of each ear of corn).

Once the crop matured the six rows of the cross-pollinated Variety B were gathered and shelled separately and sold the following year by Uncle Jim as <u>Hauk's Hybrid Seed Corn</u>. All the remaining two rows of Variety A were gathered and sold just like any other self-pollinated corn. I love this story because I think it took a lot of courage for a small country store-owner to initiate a seed corn project like this. It was a successful enterprise for quite a few years.

Aunt Clara and Uncle Jim actually lived, with their two daughters, in the same building as their store. Their living room was next to the front door of the store so if they were in the house portion of the building they could just walk through a door into the store and wait on customers. If you wanted something you thought they didn't have, you could ask, and they just might walk into a storeroom at the back of the store and bring it out.

Hauk's Hybrid Seed Corn Sack

Another difference between then and now was most rural people bought groceries on credit. Farmers' incomes could be pretty lean in the spring and summer and folks just bought groceries and settled up at the end of the month. If they could not pay their bill at the end of the month, the store might have to carry it over until after the harvest. Of course, there were a few people who never paid and that debt had to be written off as a loss after a few years. We raised so much of what we ate that, after selling our extra eggs to the store, our food bill was only a few dollars a month for all six of us, counting Grandma.

A little aside: The way people dressed back in the 40's and 50's is a far cry from today. A girl always wore a dress, or a blouse and skirt to school—be it in the first grade, junior high, high school or college. And she did not have shorts on under the skirt, even in elementary school. Boys wore blue jeans to school all the way through high school. In Rosebud most junior high and high school boys cuffed their pants leg up twice. That was cool. Men's Wrangler Jeans today are still cut pretty much like they were when I was a kid. Women's jeans have changed. They were high waisted with the zipper up the side. I think this was to make their stomach look as flat as possible. But I am a boy, so what would I know? No boy, school age or older, wore shorts—ever. Not even Bermuda shorts. They did not yet exist where we lived.

Both men and women often wore hats. Women wore hats to church and they could be very fancy. When Mom worked outside in the summer she would put on a sunbonnet to protect her skin from the sun. Of course she made her own bonnets. I suspect most people have never seen a sunbonnet except in pictures of pioneers in covered wagons. Men usually wore straw hats when they worked outside in the summertime. We three boys got a new straw hat at Aunt Clara's store at the beginning of each summer, and they would be totally trashed by the time school started. Men usually wore felt hats when they wore a suit or even when they just went to town on Saturday afternoon. Stetson was the brand of choice. Men often wore caps with fur flaps when they were outside in the winter.

On cold days we would pull those flaps down and our frozen ears were much warmer.

What about girls' swimsuits? I'm really not qualified to talk about them since I never went to a swimming pool until I was almost in high school, but why stop when I'm on a roll? Even the modest two-piece swimsuits, much less bikinis, weren't worn outside of Hollywood yet. A girl wearing one would have been considered scandalous. And cut up above the thigh? You gotta be kidding! The bottom of the swimsuit was cut straight across the bottom and even that was a bit risqué. Any Texas girl would have been horrified at the mere though of a swimsuit that consisted of four triangles of materials held together by thin ties. Even this farm boy's wildest fantasy couldn't have envisioned such a thing.

I was out at Hobby Airport in Houston on a Friday afternoon at rush hour recently and I decided to observe what women are wearing today just to verify my memories about the differences in how they dress today from back then. The airport was jammed with people and I observed just how many women had on a dress or a skirt. I knew this custom had changed a lot but I was shocked by what I actually observed. Of the hundreds and hundreds of girls and women at the airport, I saw less than a dozen women in skirts.

I have no way to back up this statement but I believe, if I had observed the same crowd back in 1950, I probably would **not** have seen a single woman who was not in a dress or skirt at a place like an airport. People dressed more formally for all occasions back then and people traveling on an airplane would have dressed in their best "Sunday go to meetin' clothes." Men would have worn suits and hats and women, dresses, hose, and heels.

Now even though I said clothes were a lot more conservative way back then, girls did have short shorts. I recall going to a Little League game one night when I was in about the ninth grade and Bea Baca was there to watch her little brother Mike play ball. Well, Bea was wearing some short shorts that I remember even today. I wonder why I would have noticed that? I'm pretty sure it couldn't have been hormones or puberty because we discussed everything at our kitchen table and those words were never mentioned.

> Country Boy Good Food Tip: Find vegetables and fruit that were ripened on the vine (or tree) even it you might have to cut out a bad spot. The flavor is amazing compared to what they pick green and sell at the grocery store today.

Lone Star Quilt
Cotton Samples, Carding Combs

History Lesson #11.
Quilting and the Garden

When the cotton was ginned a quarter pound sample from each bale was sent to Austin to be graded. The price that the bale of cotton would bring was partially determined by the quality of the cotton. The two measures of quality were staple and grade. The staple was the length of the individual cotton strands. Our cotton averaged a 3/4-inch staple. You have probably heard that cotton from the Nile River area in Egypt is better than cotton from the USA. That is because cotton from the Nile River basin had a staple of one inch or more.

The grade was how clean the cotton was. The unused portion of the cotton sample was mailed back to the farmer with a green grade card stating the grade and staple for that bale of cotton. One memorable cotton grade is "Fair to Middling." When you ask a country boy how he is doing he might answer, "Fair to Middling." I bet you didn't know where that expression came from!

Once the farmer received the unused portion of the cotton sample back from Austin, the ladies would use that cotton to make batting for quilts. The batting is the filling between the quilt top and the backing of the quilt that makes the quilt thick enough to keep you warm. First the cotton had to be combed. We had a special tool to comb the cotton and that was often my job. We could comb the cotton and listen to a radio show like "The Shadow Knows" or "Henry! Henry Aldridge!" Or maybe a soap opera like my Mother's favorite, "Stella Dallas."

I believe a soap opera on the radio was only 15 minutes long each day. If she missed a week or two of the story while we were picking cotton Mom would pick up the plot with no trouble at all the next time she listened. There were probably six or eight soap operas each day. Mother always listened to Stella Dallas while she ironed.

It took two combs to comb the cotton. As you can see in the picture a comb was a thin piece of wood about 4 inches by 10 inches that had a handle. The bristles on each comb were made from hundreds of short wires. I would take a small handful of cotton and brush it on the bristles of both combs. The two combs were dragged across the cotton in opposite directions several times. The result was a 4-inch by 10-inch layer of very smooth cotton that was used as batting in the quilts.

Each winter my Mother dragged out her home made quilting frame and set it up in the living room. She had saved scrap material all year long and pieced it together into pretty quilt patterns like a "Double Wedding Ring" or "Log Cabin." I don't know when she found time to sew all those small pieces of fabric together with all the other jobs she did. But like magic, each winter, several quilt tops would appear already pieced together.

Mom and Grandma would roll the front and backside of the quilt onto the quilting frame with the batting in the middle. Then they would sit and hand stitch the quilt together for many long hours. That stitching of the three layers together is the process known as quilting. They would make one or two quilts each winter. After we were married Anne and I once counted 33 quilts in my parents' home.

Mother had some uses for quilts that were normal for her but were heretical for city folks who pamper their quilts. To Mom quilts weren't only for show. They were also functional. She would place an "old quilt" she considered worn out between the bedsprings and the mattress so rust from the bedsprings would get on the quilt and not on the mattress. When Mom and Dad slaughtered a calf they would sometimes give half of it to us. But they didn't want the frozen meat to melt while we drove the 150 miles from Rosebud to Houston so Dad would put the meat in a washtub in the trunk and Mother would sometimes wrap the tub in an old quilt. Anne usually "forgot" to return those old beat up quilts to my Mother.

Mother entered several of the quilts she made into the Heart of Texas Fair in Waco and after success there she entered a few of her quilts in the

State Fair in Dallas. She won a couple of Blue Ribbons and several Red Ribbons. Her workmanship was exceptional and I believe she got a ribbon for every quilt she ever entered in a Fair. After Mom died, David's wife, Sharon, and my wife, Anne, finished stitching the ribbing around the outer edge of the last quilt Mom had been working on. That quilt was entered in the Heart of Texas Fair in Waco and predictably—won a ribbon also.

As much time as quilting took, the garden took much more effort from Mother and Grandma. We had a garden that was about a half acre. That is probably bigger than two city lots. To say we raised almost everything we ate would be an understatement. Remember all of those chickens we raised each year. We also milked our own cow, gathered our own eggs, and took one of the heifers to the slaughterhouse when fresh beef was needed. Except for flour, coffee, sugar, and spices we got almost all of the rest of the food we ate from the garden. Mother even made her own ketchup and sauerkraut. I was "allowed" to work in the garden quite a bit.

So what did we grow in our garden? We grew just about everything we ate—potatoes, green beans, pinto beans, black eyed peas, English peas, tomatoes, okra, lettuce, cabbage, cucumbers, both to eat and for making pickles, dill (the herb you put in the dill pickle jar with the cucumbers), onions, bell peppers, poppies (for poppy seed kolaches), beets, and turnips.

The vegetables from your grocery store's produce department don't hold a candle to Mom's garden fresh vegetables. In addition to the garden we had a long row of blackberry bushes in the middle of one of the fields. Peach, fig, and pear trees produced fruit Mom used to make preserves and jellies. We harvested and froze enough corn from our cornfields to provide us with corn year around. When I was little, before the freezers, Mother canned everything from the garden. Canning was a whole other major process.

Mother continued canning some things even after we had a freezer. One of those was dill pickles. Her pickles were as good as any I have ever tasted! After we boys grew up and married, she would make extra pickles to share with our families. Any meal tasted better with Mom's pickles as a side dish and a sandwich made using those pickles was incomparable! My mouth is watering as I remember how good those pickles were.

We would grow enough potatoes to last an entire year, and we ate potatoes just about every day. Mom would buy a few newly harvested potatoes for planting. She would cut a potato into pieces with one eye in each piece. I suspect that many people who haven't grown vegetables have never even noticed that each potato has multiple eyes. When Mom planted each piece of potato a potato plant would grow from the eye. Each potato plant would produce five or six full size potatoes.

When the new crop of potatoes was just getting mature we would go out and dig around the roots looking for full size potatoes to eat that day. We would take them to Mom and she would cook them for the noon meal. When the entire potato crop was ready to harvest Dad would put one plow on the tractor and come into the garden and plow up one row of potatoes at a time. Then we would each take a bucket and go pick up the potatoes, being careful to knock the excess dirt off of each one. The harvested potatoes needed to be stored someplace that was cool and dry. For us, that was under the house. We would spread them out so most of them did not touch one another. This was because if one potato became rotten, it would usually make any potato touching it rotten, as in "one rotten apple spoils the whole barrel."

Then every four or five days Mother would hand me a dishpan and send me under the house to fill it with potatoes. One unpleasant aspect of this chore was the possibility of sinking my fingers or knee into a mushy rotten potato, which felt nasty and left a stink that was hard to get rid of. I was also a little scared that I would run into a snake under there but I never did—not even once!

So how much work did it take to have a very large garden? It took a lot! First Dad would plow the garden late in the winter, kill all of the weeds and make rows. We called this bedding the land. In the early spring we would then plant the different vegetables in those rows. We would dig a shallow trench on the top of a row, drop the seeds in the trench one at a time, cover them with dirt and pat them down so the ground would retain enough moisture for the seeds to germinate. When the weeds also came up, we had to use a hoe to chop them out. Otherwise, someone had to get down on their hands and knees and pull up the weeds.

But the real work was when the vegetables got ripe. First you had to harvest them by hand and Mom would prepare some of them to be eaten that day but most of them were canned or frozen. And that was a lot of work because a large garden produces a lot of food. Mom and Grandma would work steady from early in the morning until mid-afternoon picking, cleaning, and putting up the ripe vegetables "three or four days a week, all summer long!"

Usually one or more of us boys would also be put to work helping Mom. But we really did eat great food! I didn't realize until years later how much tastier and healthier that home grown food actually was. I have never understood why a commercial food processing company like Green Giant doesn't harvest vine ripened vegetables and can or freeze them so they tasted as good as Mom's, but they don't even come close. If they sold vine-ripened vegetables they would quickly put all of their competition out of business.

I still find it amusing that as a small boy I looked forward to eating Rainbow Bread instead of having to eat Mother's homemade bread. I must point out that Mom's homemade bread did not have any preservatives and was a bit dried out by the fourth day.

Rosebud's town slogan: Everything's Rosy in Rosebud
The city government encouraged everyone in town to plant a rosebush. They must have succeeded since Rosebud, Texas is in Ripley's Believe-It-or-Not as the only town in the country with a rosebush in ever yard.

David with Tricycle and Homemade Wagon

History Lesson #12.
Saturday Afternoon in Town

Dad would work on the farm on Saturday morning but if he wasn't planting or harvesting, he took Saturday afternoon off and went to town. Starting at an early age, maybe 8 or 9, I would go to town with him. He would
begin at some place like the cotton gin where he might need to pay for ginning cotton, he might need to buy fertilizer, or he might just wanted to sit
and chat. There would always be a couple of other farmers sitting around
talking about farming. how rain was affecting farming, or what politicians
were doing to cheat the farmers.

They might talk about what kind of hybrid seed they had used and how
it worked, what they were going to plant, why, and when. Or perhaps they
talked about terracing the land, the price of a tractor, a new type plow or
combine—but even if they strayed off the subject for a few minutes they
always quickly returned to some aspect of farming. I might have been
bored but I pretty much understood whatever they were talking about.

One interesting person who was often at the gin was Monroe Parcus.
Monroe was the gin's intelligent bookkeeper who ran the office, resolving
touchy misunderstandings good-naturedly. This was important, because
the gin operated 24 hours a day during ginning season and confusion
about things occurred regularly. One thing that made Monroe hard to go
unnoticed was his weight. He weighed around 600 pounds. When he sent
someone to get him a meal at the Dairy King, they brought it back in a
large dishpan.

As a young boy, the highlight of my weekend was going to the picture
show, which always had a good western "shoot'em up" movie on Saturday
afternoon. Dad would give me a quarter and drop me off near the theater.
My brothers did not go to the movies with me because we were such dif-

ferent ages they would be doing something else. The theater did not have any concessions other than a penny gumball machine but there was a man three doors down who sold popcorn. There was only one size. It was a small bag and cost a nickel. So, of course, I started there. The movie cost nine cents and obviously the left over penny went into the penny gum machine. We could chew it as soon as we finished our popcorn.

We all crowded as close to the front row as possible. One of the people who went to the movies with us on Saturday afternoon was Cornbread. Cornbread was about 30 years old and quite a bit overweight himself. He never held a job as far as I knew and didn't have anything to do. He really enjoyed going to the Saturday afternoon movie with us kids. He always got a seat on the end of the front row. He would lead the cheers when the good guy came riding around the corner to the rescue and he helped lead the boos when the hero kissed the girl.

The movies had heroes like Hop-A-Long Cassidy, Lash LaRue, or the Lone Ranger with his horse Silver. The Lone Ranger used silver bullets in his pistol and his Indian sidekick Tonto's horse was a paint named Scout.

Gene Autry and his horse, Champion, or perhaps Roy Rogers and his horse, Trigger were other western movie heroes. Roy Rogers' movies always included Dale Evans and her horse, Buttermilk. She would always end up as Roy Rogers' girl friend. When they kissed, we would all boo. Roy's dog was Bullet and his sidekick was Jingles. Jingles was jolly and good for a lot of laughs. Jingles had a jeep named Nellie Bell. The good guy would go into the saloon and order a sarsaparilla. The bad guy would already be there drinking whiskey. A fight would then break out between the good guy and the bad guy.

Dad would laugh about the western movies. He said it didn't make any difference who was in the movie, the good guy with the white hat would be riding his horse chasing the bad guy—and they always rode around the same rock. When the movie was over I still had a dime and I might get a nickel RC Cola or a nickel Baby Ruth at the five and dime store. Or I might just save part of it.

The Rosebud storeowners gave people tickets when they bought something in town and on Saturday afternoon at 4:00 I would find Dad at the weekly drawing. They gave a nice prize each Saturday, maybe $150 or so, but you had to be present to win so just about everybody came. Since Dad was buying high cost equipment like tractors and farm tools he had a lot of tickets with his name on them and stood a decent chance of winning.

If Dad hadn't gotten everything done before the drawing, afterwards he might take me and go by the local tractor dealer or an auto dealer and bargain with the owner for a new car or tractor. It was very boring and I would wander off, but I got to watch him conduct his business first hand. I don't think it ever occurred to Mom or Dad that they might want to keep things from us like what they paid for cars or farm machinery.

One year the Chamber of Commerce in Rosebud came up with the idea to do something a little different. Instead of holding the usual Saturday afternoon drawing before Thanksgiving, they decided they would throw about 15 live turkeys off the top of the two-story City Hall building. It was not a pretty sight! People went a little crazy trying to capture the turkeys as they sailed down and in a lot of cases several people would get hold of a different part of the same bird. I think a few of the turkeys died right then and there. Needless to say, they never threw live turkeys off of City Hall again.

As a kid, I was fascinated with the Kirkscey Meat Locker Plant. Individuals rented lockers there to store their frozen meat. The lockers were stacked one on top of another, five high, and as the name implies, each locker came with a key and was kept locked. According to Mr. Kirkscey, the lockers were a little over three cubic feet; the lower ones had a door while the upper lockers had sliding trays.

Ours was one of the higher ones so Dad would have to move the ladder over to our locker to get the meat he wanted. Just before we went home from town on Saturday afternoon we would drop by the locker plant and pick up enough meat for the following week. I would go in with Dad and once that big thick door closed behind us I felt a momentary panic that we might freeze to death if we were somehow trapped in there too long.

When our supply of beef got low Dad would select a young steer or heifer that weighted about 400 pounds and take it to the locker plant for processing. They would handle the entire slaughtering process according to my parents' specifications. After the beef was cut and double wrapped in white oily butcher paper, it would be placed in the quick-freezing room overnight.

There were several other rooms in the locker plant such as the room where they hung the sides of beef until they could get to the butchering, the cutting and wrapping room, and of course the very cold room where the meat lockers were. The locker plant only got 4 cents per pound back in the early days for the entire process ($16 for a 400 pound animal which would yield about 140 pounds of packaged beef). Mr. Kirkscey said that a big profit maker came from selling the cowhides to some people from Ft. Worth for anywhere from $10 to $60 per hide.

One more interesting detail is a government health inspector forced Mr. Kirkscey to close the locker plant in 1974. A site was selected and a new locker was built with a retail department, where he sold all kinds of beef, pork, bacon, ham, and lots of excellent Kirkscey smoked sausage. The new locker was operated as a custom processing plant for about 20 years.

However, many people had freezers at home by this time so they were no longer using many of the lockers. The new locker plant was finally sold to investors taking advantage of a government subsidy for processing Emus. Since the main purpose of that venture was to get the government subsidy, and Emu processing was never much of a success, the plant was soon closed. Today both the old and new locker plants are in ruins.

One Saturday, when I was a freshman in high school, Dad came home from town in stitches. He just couldn't stop laughing. He had seen something right in the middle of downtown Rosebud that was the funniest thing he had ever seen. The local lumberyard manager, George Stock, actually went out in public wearing pants that were cut off at the knees. Can you imagine how silly that looked to a farmer like Dad?

Since I never once saw Dad in a short sleeve shirt, no never, not even at home, I guess he thought short pants were unbelievable. Everyone but Dad wore short sleeve shirts. People were always giving them to him as presents but when he passed away he had several drawers full of them that were still in their wrappers. When he wanted to be casual, he would roll up the cuffs two turns on each sleeve of his long sleeve shirt. But for a grown man to wear pants out in public that were cut off at the knees was so unexpected that he laughed about it for days.

> Country Boy Observation: Every where I turn people are screaming about Immigration, Abortion, Gun Control and other issues they think are dooming America to eternal damnation. What I don't understand is why more people don't support voting the politicians out of office for passing legislation they find objectionable.

Grandpa Skupin, Robert and Dad

History Lesson #13.
Grandpa Skupin

We lived on one side of Rosebud and Dad's parent's Grandpa, Henry Skupin, and Grandmother, Agnes Reznicek, lived about the same distance on the other side of town. Dad's parents had come over from Czechoslovakia separately and met in El Campo, Texas. In order to escape seven years conscription in the Kaiser's army, Grandpa walked 400 miles across Germany and stowed away on a ship in Hamburg that landed in Galveston, Texas in 1907.

He left home in the middle of the night without telling his friends or family what he was doing. When he reached the port in Hamburg he noticed some vendors selling oranges, so he bought their oranges and talked his way onto the ship, posing as an orange vendor selling oranges to the passengers. Once aboard he hid until they were out at sea.

Grandmother Skupin came over with her brother Charlie in a ship that landed in Corpus Christi. She spoke Czech and never learned to speak English. Obviously Dad and his brothers and sisters spoke Czech in their home.

After I became an adult I was told that my Grandmother Skupin would not allow my Mother in her house because Mom was a German. Prejudices are everywhere and frequently crop up in unexpected places. I never felt like I knew Grandmother very well. It probably didn't help that Mother wasn't welcome in her home so I suspect I didn't go over there very much. I remember being a small child and unable to communicate with her.

I find it interesting to contrast attitudes today vs. attitudes when Dad's parents came to this county. Grandpa's first name was Heinrich but when he came through customs in Galveston the official who filled out his immigration papers listed him as Henry. When Grandmother Skupin came through customs her first name was Anezka, but the official who filled out her immigration papers listed her name as Annie. Back in those days people wanted very badly to fit in, so Grandpa and Grandma kept the Americanized names, Henry and Annie. Later Grandma decided she liked the sound of the name Agnes better than Annie, so she was known as Agnes after that.

Grandmother Skupin drowned before dawn one morning in a stock tank when I was eight. No one knows what she was doing anywhere near that tank that early in the day. Also, I am told that Grandmother was a very proud person and was better educated than Grandpa even though she never learned to speak English.

She did write articles in Czech for the Czechoslovakian SPJST newspaper, the Vesnick, which my parents received once a month. Mom and Dad never taught us any foreign languages because they were afraid they would confuse us. Well maybe a few foreign words snuck in there occasionally. When we were small children they would tickle our tummies and point out our "pupek" (the Czech word for naval.)

Grandpa was trained as a blacksmith before he came to America and someone with those skills could earn a decent living over here. He made the 150-mile trip from Rosebud to Houston each winter for supplies. He used a wagon pulled by two mules and the trip took about a month.

Most of the work he did for farmers was on credit and when the depression hit in 1929 the farmers could not pay what they owed him. Apparently things got pretty tough financially in the Skupin household, as they were many places during the Great Depression.

Around Rosebud there were at least three SPJST Lodges where I regularly went to dances when I was in high school. So what is an SPJST Lodge? Well, the letters SPJST are the first letters of Czechoslovakian words that roughly translate to "Benevolent Society of Czechoslovakian People of Texas."

Dad had a sister who was stillborn and a brother Frank who died of dehydration at the age of one. Perhaps due to the memory of these deaths, Mom and Dad bought each of us a $1,000 SPJST Life Insurance Policy that could pay for our funeral if we should die in childhood. Since it was paid up, I still have that policy.

One of the largest SPJST Halls in Texas is three miles from where I live here in the Houston Heights. I still go to certain functions there and receive my SPJST calendar in the mail each year. When I asked my Aunt Jodie where my grandparents met, she just giggled and said she imagined it was at one of those SPJST dance halls.

A little aside: when I was young and someone died, a relative would stay at the funeral home with the body until it was buried. But a lot of times the adults had to work. I remember being left alone in the funeral home "overnight" with both Grandpa Skupin's and Grandma Engbrock's bodies when they passed away. Even though they had both been very important to me and I loved them, those nights were still extremely long and boring and this tradition has now gone away.

A lot of people retired back to Rosebud so we had more funerals in the area than you would expect. We went to quite a few funerals each year and my Dad was a pallbearer in many of them. I decided early on that a funeral was a kind of party. The cause of the gathering was sobering, but the only times you got to see all of these special friends and relatives were funerals and weddings. It was more like a quiet party in memory of the deceased rather than something totally tragic. At my age, I have now also been a pallbearer quite a few times.

One thing that can make a funeral really sad is when very few people come. It seems to me as if city folks are afraid of funerals. Maybe they are afraid of their own mortality. I suspect that most of my friends who were raised in big cities may not average getting to one funeral a year. But our presence at funerals is very important to grieving relatives who are trying to come to grips with the loss of their loved ones. I know how comforting it was for us boys when the church was full at both Mom's and Dad's funerals.

Small towns still observe this special occasion in much the same way it has been observed traditionally. The women of the church prepare a noon meal on the day of the funeral for the relatives and out of town friends of the deceased. Most of their friends and relatives attend the service. Drivers meeting the funeral procession stop their cars, get out, and stand beside them, even if they don't have a clue who the deceased is. These gestures of respect are very moving and have been mostly lost in large cities.

Back to the subject of Grandpa and life as a Skupin in Texas. Grandpa was paranoid that the Germans were going to come to Texas and take him back to Germany. The Germans ruled Czechoslovakia when he left there in 1907. I was told that Germans were paid better than Czechoslovakians and Grandpa spoke German well enough that he passed for a German and was paid German wages when he worked in a locomotive factory. The letters he wrote to his family back home, even after being in America for 45 years, never revealed very much because he was still afraid the Germans might try to come and get him.

After Grandmother passed away, all of the Skupin offspring would often gather to visit at Grandpa's on Sunday afternoon. You have probably never come across a gathering of people who shared a common background, yet were more diverse.

First let's name the players. Mother and Dad were the eldest Skupins and Aunt Tillie (Dad's sister) and her husband, Uncle Charles Engel, were the next in line. Uncle Charlie (Dad's brother) with his wife, Aunt Jodie Chisholm, and Aunt Mary (Dad's youngest sister) and her husband, Uncle Bill Surovik, rounded out the Skupin aunts and uncles. That is correct, there was an Uncle Charles and an Uncle Charlie, so don't get confused.

At these Sunday gatherings Dad only wanted to talk farming. Uncle Charles was an avid educator, what we might call an "activist" today, who wrote letters to his congressmen and even to the President of the United States voicing his opinions, so he wanted to talk about politics and education. Uncle Charlie was a "jack-of-all-trades," but unlike the saying—"jack-of-all-trades, master of none," he was diverse but quite successful. All five of his kids have college degrees. Uncle Bill was an accountant in Dallas and loved music.

The wives would go into one room and the men would go into another room and try to be civil to each other even though each of the four men totally disagreed with one another. It soon turned into a hollering match each week. Except for Grandpa. He mostly just relit his pipe, took another draw on it, and listened.

Aunt Tillie and Uncle Charles lived about five miles North of Rosebud on a small farm near Travis. Just a detail, but Uncles Charles, in addition to being married to Dad's sister, was also Mother's cousin. Very few people took education more seriously than my Uncle Charles. He was a Falls County school supervisor. I really don't know exactly what all he did but I do know that he taught Number Sense and Slide Rule at Rosebud High for Interscholastic League. His students would often win first at the state competition.

Tillie and Charles' daughter Peggy won state in Slide Rule in her sophomore year and was not allowed to compete again because she had already won. One year Robert was on Uncle Charles' slide rule team and won third, behind two other Rosebud boys, at both district and bi-district. Robert had a conflict so he skipped the state meet, even though he qualified. He assumed the competition would be pretty stiff at the state championship level. But again the two other boys from Rosebud won first and second at the state meet so he very well may have won third if he had gone.

Aunt Tillie, a beautician, seemed to let Uncle Charles make most family decisions, but after he retired, he had a stroke and she took charge just like someone who had always run things. I enjoyed watching her manage her own life and his so competently when circumstances made it necessary.

When I say Uncle Charlie was a jack-of-all-trades just what do I mean? Well he made his living at one time or another farming, running a country store, remodeling kitchens, painting houses, cleaning carpets, and finally settling on an exterminating business and cleaning septic tanks in Brownfield, Texas, where Aunt Jodie grew up.

He was one of the more innovative people I have come across. I remember him having a house he used for an office that he painted in black and yellow stripes with three-foot high bugs hanging out the second floor windows advertising his exterminating business. He also bought an old Renault Dauphine with a sunroof at the junkyard. He put a hot water heater though the sunroof, put a head on the hot water heater to make it look like a giant bug—painted his name and business on the side of the car—and put it beside the road outside of town as another advertisement.

When their home got a little crowded with five kids Uncle Charlie encouraged his eldest son, Mike, to dig a hole under the house and live in his homemade basement. Then, just for fun, the door that led to the new basement was a secret panel in a kitchen cabinet like in a James Bond movie. On top of taking care of their large family, Aunt Jodie was also Uncle Charlie's entire office staff. All kids loved being around Uncle Charlie and Aunt Jodie.

Aunt Mary was married to Uncle Bill, who used his G I Bill to get a degree in accounting from SMU. Uncle Bill had an unbelievable amount of energy. I don't think it was uncommon for him to stay up until 2:00 AM or even later, all of his life. One of his quirks that I found amusing was that he talked very fast. He was so excited about what he wanted to say that the words just tumbled out.

One story about him is that he played a pretty mean piano back in high school. One night he was at a dance hall in Burlington and the band's piano player was sick, so the bandleader asked if anyone would like to sit in and play piano for them that night. After that night Uncle Bill became the band's regular piano player for a couple of years. One thing Aunt Mary and Uncle Bill liked to do was go dancing. They continued to dance regularly until their health failed and they were no longer able to get out.

They stayed in Dallas after Uncle Bill graduated from SMU and were our city relatives. Aunt Mary worked for the head of the Math Department at SMU and I remember her being terrified that they were going to make her convert to using a word processor instead of her beloved IBM Selectric typewriter. A short time later, she was telling me how much she loved her word processor.

Rosebud has a Golden Years Reunion each year. Anyone who graduated from Rosebud High more than 50 years ago is invited. That is a great way to have a reunion because students in a small high school like Rosebud socialize with people a couple of grades on either side of themselves. About 350 people return each year and have a great time. Aunt Mary and Uncle Bill never failed to attend. I look forward to getting to go myself in 2010.

According to Aunt Mary's son, Howard, Uncle Charlie had an interest in spiders. So, when Mary saw an opportunity to help with his hobby she did so by bringing him a tarantula. Assuming he wanted it alive she found one and coaxed it onto a stick before putting it into a jar to bring it home. It wasn't until she presented it to him and he warned her of the danger, that she realized a tarantula has a pretty nasty bite.

You wouldn't think the sport of boxing would attract the Skupin family crowd. You could not be more wrong. Lott, eight miles north of Rosebud, had an outdoor boxing ring and was a hotbed of boxing entertainment. It was the idea of a man named Judge Haley who owned the local dry goods store. Some of you may have shopped in his western store, which became immensely popular for its low price boots and jeans after the movie "Urban Cowboy" with John Travolta came out in the 1970's.

The Lott boxing ring was an outdoor wooden platform with no seating and stood about four feet off of the ground with three ropes on each side just like on TV. It even had overhead lights. Guys would get together, the competitive spirit would overcome their good sense and a match would be set. Come Saturday night they would get in the ring with their seconds and after instructions from the referee, they would come out fighting. After three, two-minute rounds, the referee would declare a winner. His decision was final.

Charlie Skupin and Alvin Lueke had a hotly contested match one Saturday night and Uncle Charlie lost. Charlie then built a practice ring at home and also trained at the YMCA in Temple where he boxed with sparring partners and he defeated a member of the University of Texas boxing team by a decision. Charlie would run a couple of miles every morning before breakfast and consume enormous portions of oatmeal and other foods. To make a long story short, Charlie won the return match with Lueke but when Robert ran into Lueke a couple of years ago at a Bigler-Neumann (Grandma Engbrock's family) reunion, Lueke felt that they tied since he had won once and Charlie had won once.

Uncle Charlie then fought in the Golden Gloves competition at the Dallas Athletic Club. Dad and several of Charlie's local friends, including his second, Jerry Lanicek, were in attendance. According to Dad, Charlie was knocked out in the first round. That ended Charlie's boxing except for a couple of bouts in the South Pacific while serving in U. S. Army during WWII where he defeated the island's most notable native boxer by a decision. Uncle Charlie is 89 today and sharp as a tack.

On holidays all of the Skupins would often come to our house for dinner. When Mother wasn't very busy she would serve dinner at 12:00 noon. On washday she would serve dinner at 12:00 noon. When she had to work in the garden, prepare chickens for freezing, or butcher a hog—she would serve dinner at 12:00 noon. So naturally she would prepare dinner to serve at 12:00 noon for her Sunday guests. Most of the relatives would start arriving about 10:30 and the other wives all pitched in to help get the meal ready.

Unfortunately Uncle Bill and Aunt Mary just didn't seem to be able to get there from Dallas until about 12:45. Mom would start looking out her kitchen window for the Suroviks about a quarter to twelve. We could see company coming for about a half mile and as the minutes clicked by with no Suroviks in sight, Mom would start squirming. And when Mom squirmed we all squirmed.

My mom could really cook! She started with almost all fresh grown food and freshly baked bread and pies. She would often prepare more than a dozen different dishes. Even if there were going to be more than 20 for dinner she would just prepare another dish rather than make huge amounts of any one kind of food.

With our family, when you served yourself seconds it was poor manners to take all that was left. Why? Because if you took all of the remaining mashed potatoes, for instance, and someone else wanted more mashed potatoes they would be all gone. So even if there weren't many mashed potatoes left, you only took half and left the rest for the next person. Then at the end of the meal Mom frantically tried to get someone to finish every bit of food left on the table. "We'll have good weather if you finish the mashed potatoes," she would implore.

When my Grandpa got older and we got a telephone, my Dad would call him each morning before he went to the fields to work just to be sure Grandpa was ok. One morning, when I was in early high school, Dad called and no one answered. After trying several times Dad asked me to take the pickup and go by before school and make sure Grandpa was all right.

David probably rode with me and we got quite a shock when we got there. Grandpa was lying on the front porch. He'd had a stroke and had fallen and could not get up—nor did he have the strength to drag himself to the telephone. What happened after we found our Grandpa that morning seems to have been pretty much erased from my memory.

I would have called home and told Mom who would then have gotten Dad out of the field. Then I believe I got Grandpa into the pickup and drove him to Sweptson's hospital. But to tell the truth I have no memory of just what took place. We may have called an ambulance, but I doubt it. I guess the trauma of finding him like that blanked my memory out. I do know that when Grandpa recovered enough to get out of the hospital, he went into a nursing home where he lived for three or four more years. He was mentally alert and we visited him often but he never walked again.

Dad was the first born child and the next oldest was his brother Henry. When Henry was 18 he developed a malignant abdominal tumor and in those days they had no treatment for cancer. He was sent home to die and I don't think he lived very long after that. I am told that my Dad was very close to Henry and it was quite hard on him when Henry passed away. Obviously I am named for both Grandpa and the Uncle Henry I never knew.

Skupin Parking Privileges: This is the right to expect a parking spot near the door to the place you are going. You won't ever get that spot if you take the first open place you find in the back of the parking lot. Visit the Skupin Mecca (Rosebud) and maybe you too will be granted these parking privileges!

Henry in a Rare Icestorm

History Lesson #14.
Milking Cows & Other Chores

Most farmers raised at least a few cows because almost all farms had some land that wasn't good for crops but would be just fine for a pasture. Each farmer also usually had one bull. Farmers would often have 20 to 50 cows plus their calves. Ranchers, on the other hand, might have hundreds of cows, and only have enough cropland to grow hay for their cattle. Most farmers would select one or two cows to milk. Jersey cows were usually preferred because they gave lots of milk with a high cream content. Since you wanted milk year around, you hoped all of the milk-producing cows did not have their calves at the same time of the year.

Dad would do the morning milking before breakfast. The cows had to be milked twice each day, and I do mean <u>every single day</u>. That included Sundays, holidays, rainy days, or even in the snow. You had to milk the cows twice a day and feed the chickens, cattle, and the pets every day. Farmers almost never did anything frivolous like go on vacation.

When the milk cows gave birth, the newborn calf was brought to the barn and penned up. The cow was turned out each morning and would graze in the pastures near the barn throughout the day. But when the cow's milk bag (or udder) got full in the afternoon she would come to the barn to nurse her calf. The calf was given access to the mother and would be allowed to nurse for a minute or two until the mother's milk began to flow freely. We referred to this as the cow letting her "milk drop." The calf would be tied off and we would milk a little over half of the mother's milk. Then the calf would be released to suckle the rest of the mother's milk.

Later the mother and calf would be kept in separate pens overnight so the mother could be milked again in the morning before the calf got it all. The mother cow would be given hay each night to help her produce a lot of milk. After the morning milking, the cow would again be released into the pasture for the day. When the calf got a few months old the mother cow would quit coming to the barn each evening to feed her calf. When I was as young as 6 or 7 it was my job to go out in the pasture and drive the mother milk cow back to the barn so she would be there when Dad or my older brother was ready to do the milking.

Once I reached about 13 years of age it was my job to do the evening milking. When one squeezes the cow's teat, the milk would squirt into the bucket hard enough to create foam on top of the milk much like the foam when you pour a coke into a glass too quickly. Sometime the cow would swat flies with her dirty tail or kick unwanted "things" that would drop on top of the foam in the milk bucket, I would reach in and flick out the manure or whatever because I did not want my parents to know I had allowed stuff to fall into the milk. Actually, I have always suspected Dad did the same. But we never talked about it. Especially not with Mom.

And how do you milk a cow? There are several ways. Dad placed the cow's teat between his thumb and his first two fingers. He pushed his thumb and fingers together tightly as he pulled downward to squeeze the cow's teat and strip the milk out.

My hands weren't strong enough to do that so I put my entire hand around the cow's teat and closed the top finger and the thumb so the milk could only flow down. Then I squeezed the next finger and the next finger until I squeezed the milk out in the same hard stream that Dad achieved. I would squeeze one hand and then while I relaxed that hand I would squeeze the other hand. Once I had milked those two teats for a while I switched and milked the other two until all four teats had been milked.

A cowlick is that spot on your head where the hair grows the wrong way and will not lay down smoothly when you comb it. Many of us do have a cowlick or two. A cow would often licked her young calf while you were milking her just like a cat will lick her kittens. And when I walked up near the cow's head, to untie the calf after I finished milking, she would often turn her head and give me a lick or two, on my arm, with her huge tongue. I bet you have been licked by a cat but you haven't been really licked until you get licked by a cow. It will do everything but take the skin off of your bones.

Cows have really strong tongues because they tear the grass off with them when they graze rather than biting it off with their teeth as goats and horses do. It is easy to see how our ancestors might imagine that a cow licking there children's head could cause the hair to grow in the wrong direction.

Milk fresh from the cow is not homogenized and the cream separates easily; simply because the oil based cream will rise to the top of the more watery milk. We poured the whole milk (obviously whole milk is milk that still has the cream in it) into a separator to stand overnight giving the cream time to rise. The separator was not refrigerated. It was a tin cylinder about 2 feet tall, had a diameter of about 14 inches and stood on tall wooden legs. The lower part of the separator was funnel shaped with a spigot on the bottom. The cream would rise to the top and the milk would be drained out of the spigot at the bottom.

Some of the cream that remained would be placed in a butter churn and I might be "allowed" to churn the cream into homemade butter. All you had to do to make butter from the cream was turn the crank on the churn for 15 to 20 minutes. This left us with a lump of butter and some watery buttermilk, which we put in the slop bucket for the hogs.

I must admit I never fully appreciated how good that cream was. There was so much of it you could never fully stir it completely into the milk and I didn't like the way flecks of cream would float in the milk. Boy, what I would give for that cream today. Once milk is homogenized, as all store bought milk is today, the cream will not separate. Another use we made of whole milk was to make cottage cheese. Grandmother would add retin to the milk and heat it until it formed curds. Then she would place it in cheesecloth and hang it under a dripping faucet in the kitchen sink to complete the cheese making.

One chore I could do at an early age was gathering eggs each afternoon. Most of the nests were hung from the ceiling in the chicken house and I could gather those eggs quickly. One of the other nests where the hens liked to lay eggs was in a shed out by the old barn that we called the tool shed. One evening when I was reaching into that nest I spotted a snake curled up in there sleeping. Never mind that it was only a chicken snake. I did not like snakes and putting my hand within a couple of inches of one scared the heebie-jeebies out of me. Mother came out, got a hoe, and "helped me" kill that snake. Of course I stayed several steps behind her and just pointed.

Another job was to go out to the corn crib each evening, get about a dozen ears of corn, shell them in the manual hand cranked corn sheller (one ear of corn at a time) and scatter the shelled corn in front of the chicken house. The corn supplemented the store bought chicken feed that was the chickens' primary food. It was an easy job that even a youngster could do. Another thing we fed the chickens was ground oyster shells. Not a lot but enough to make the eggshell thicker and less likely to break. I found it curious that you could feed a chicken something that made the eggshells stronger. I also found it surprising how the cow's milk would taste bitter when the cow ate ragweeds.

We didn't always have pigs but when we did I often had to feed them. We kept a 5-gallon bucket in the corner of the kitchen where we threw food scraps. Remember, we had more milk and cream than we could use and we didn't always eat all of the homemade bread or cornbread that Mom made so our scraps were pretty good. My job was to carry the bucket of slop (usually about 2 gallons) all the way out to the pigpen and pour it into a trough, i.e. "Slop the Hogs."

Slop could smell a bit nasty in the summer time. Of course nothing had the kind of stench the pigpen had. While I was out there I would also go into the corncrib, get a few ears of corn, and give them to the pigs. I didn't have to shell them because there weren't many pigs to fight over the corn and they could just eat it off of the cob.

We also had several barn cats. The cats were slightly wild and we didn't really pet them. They were well fed but it was hoped they would kill a few rats and mice out in the barns, which they did. Every morning Mother would make mush for the cats and dogs. She put some lard in a fry pan with some corn meal and milk and any food scraps that were available and cooked it until it thickened like oatmeal. The pets got a hot meal every morning and they loved it.

As long as we are talking about farm animals I want to tell you about Mose Hill. Occasionally a large animal like a cow would die on the farm. For several reasons Dad did not like to just let it lie there for the buzzards to pick over. But, even for this, "Rosebud had a solution." All you had to do was call Mose Hill and within a couple of hours he would show up to haul the dead cow 35 miles to the glue factory over near Belton.

There were a couple of times I had to get into his pickup and go with him to open pasture gates and show him where the corpse was. But that pickup stunk so badly it was hard to keep my lunch down. To make matters worse he might already have a couple of dead animals in the trailer. I would stand upwind while he worked and he would be sucking vigorously on a cigar.

He would throw a chain around the dead cow and wench her into the trailer in just a few minutes. Now I know Mose washed that pickup and trailer regularly, but it smelled so rank that a city ordinance was passed defining where he could and could not park his rig. Mose Hill was a black man who filled a niche doing something nobody else would do. He also was entrepreneurial and after I left town, he moved up to become Rosebud's police chief.

I also remember working with my Uncle Charlie for a few days one summer. We were running a reaper, which is a dusty job, and it got to be lunchtime. He took me to lunch at a café in Rosebud. We dusted ourselves off as well as we could, but we had been sweating as we "bathed" in a cloud in dust all morning so we were still pretty grimy. Of course many of the business people in town were in the restaurant in suits and ties. My uncle said we shouldn't let it bother us that we weren't all that dressed up like the banker, druggist, and the other town people in the restaurant. He said to remember that we put on clean clothes that morning but the guy in the white shirt with the ring around his collar had put on a dirty shirt. My Dad never made these kinds of thought provoking social comments. This was one of the kind of things that made time spent with Uncle Charlie special.

Mom's Country Wisdom: You can lead a horse to water, but you can't make him drink.

Hand Forged, Mule Drawn Plow
Which Dad used Before I was Born

History Lesson #15.
Hauling Hay, Chopping Cotton

The most demanding physical job on the farm was hauling hay. It was so hard that by the time I got big enough to contribute Dad had decided to hire out hay hauling. The extended family in town that did the hay hauling was the Whitfields. They were three black Rosebud families and those hay haulers worked harder than anybody else I have ever seen. A bale of hay weighed between 70 and 95 pounds and you had to pick it up and throw it way up high on a trailer or pickup and then haul it to the barn. Once you got it there you had to throw the bales up into the hayloft in the barn. You did this one bale after another, hour after hour. And you think lifting weights is hard!

Now you probably wonder why I am telling you this story but you will see in a minute. Anyway, back to the Whitfields—they were all built like Arnold Schwarzenegger and they didn't need steroids. They just lifted bale after bale of hay all day long, when hay baling was in season, from the time they were about 11 years old. The young ones would drive the pickup in the field and when they got to the hayloft, they would drag the bales from the opening at the edge of the loft over to where their dad or an uncle would stack them. And their elders didn't cut them a lot of slack either.

So here is how it worked. Dad would call the head Whitfield (I think it was Roy) and say he would have approximately 500 bales in the field by noon tomorrow that needed to be hauled to the barn and put into the hayloft. They would show up with three crews who worked on commission. The more bales of hay the crew put in the loft the more the crew was paid.

It was summer time and hot, especially in the hayloft, where there was no ventilation. Each crew would rush out and take a different part of the field. The guy on the ground would trot from one bale to the next and use his hay hook to boost a bale to the man on the trailer. The guy on the trailer would reach down and slam his hay hook into the bale, and drag it up and stack it on the trailer. But only one crew at a time could unload into the hayloft in the barn and remember, they were paid by the bale. So, at some point a crew would get a little over half a load and cut and run for the barn so they would not have to wait in line to unload. In case you are wondering, a hay hook looked like Capitan Hook's artificial hand, only it had a handle. This work was harder than hard. They took some of the pain out of doing it by making a competition of it and the pay for a good crew was very high by farm labor standards.

Now here is why I am telling this story. One of the kids that grew up doing this was A. D. Whitfield, Jr. of the North Texas State "Mean Green" football team just a couple of years before Mean Joe Greene. A. D., Jr. was one fine athlete and after college he was a tailback for the Dallas Cowboys for the 1965 season. Actually he only got into a game for a couple of plays in the entire season.

The next year the Cowboys added Walt Garrison to a backfield that already had Don Perkins and Dan Reeves so Whitfield was traded to Washington where he played for the Redskins for three years. In those three years he was never the Redskins' feature back but he did average 4.4 yards per carry on 221 carries and he caught 67 passes for an average of 10.5 yards per catch. But who's counting? As far as I know that was more time in the NFL than all of the rest of the boys from Rosebud and Lott put together.

Well, unless you count LaDainian Tomlinson of the Los Angeles Chargers, who is only the best running back in the NFL. I don't think Tomlinson ever actually lived in the Rosebud School District but I have heard the NFL announcers on Monday Night Football say Tomlinson was from Rosebud, not once but twice, and how much more official than that can you get? They may have lived in the Tomlinson Hill area near Lott when he was born. Apparently his family moved to Waco when he was very young (probably before he began school) and he played high school football at Waco University High.

Of course not getting to haul hay and stack it in the barn never upset me a bit, but that doesn't mean I didn't get to feed that hay to the cows. We sometimes fed the cows in the barn, but we usually threw about eight to ten bales down from the loft into the pickup and took it to the pasture to feed them.

If I was by myself I would just point the pickup towards the middle of the pasture, put it in low-low gear and let it go wherever it went without a driver—while I got in the back and pitched the hay out on the ground, a block or two at a time, spreading it out so all of the cows could eat at once. Yes, there was a gear below low gear that was called "low-low" (also called "granny.")

Sometimes when it was muddy the pickup would slip and slide all over the dirt trail that led from the barn to the pasture. It was fun to drive in the mud and try not to get stuck in the muddy places. Mud holes gave me a good excuse to drive a little faster than usual.

Hay hauling may have been the hardest job, but I think cotton picking was next on the list. And cotton chopping was a close third. Cotton chopping was a ten-hour day and temperatures would reach the upper 90's on a central Texas afternoon in June. And there was always another row to chop. Once the cotton was planted and came up, the farmer would put the cultivator on the tractor, and plow between the rows to kill as many weeds as possible. But weeds would grow up between the stalks of cotton and you could not get them with the plow without plowing up and killing the cotton as well.

This is where the cotton hoe came in. After the farmer had cultivated, we had to walk in the freshly plowed field chopping out all of the weeds between the stalks. Now as a small fry I had helped Mom by chopping some in the garden, and I had chopped some beside my Dad. I never knew anyone that could hold a candle to Dad when it came to chopping. He could and would chop three times as fast as I no matter how hard I tried to keep up. But Mom always said a hoe handle just didn't fit very well in Dad's hand and in practice he usually seemed to have something else more important to do come chopping time. Nevertheless, when he chopped, he was a real chopping machine!

Back in those days, a lot of the seed that were planted did not germinate so there would be irregular skips between the cotton stalks. To compensate for the seed that might not come up, a farmer planted more seed than he actually wanted. On the first chopping, one of the things you had to do was "thin the cotton stalks."

We would look ahead for a gap in the stalks because we would need to leave cotton stalks next to the gaps and chop out stalks where too many had actually come up. To do this we wanted to leave three or four stalks in 6 inches. Then we wanted to chop out everything (stalks of cotton as well as the weeds) in the next six inches. And we would repeat leaving six inches of cotton followed by an empty six inches all the way down the row throughout the entire field. The objective was to kill all of the weeds while leaving only three or four healthy cotton stalks every 12 inches.

And why do you think we would remove perfectly health stalks of cotton? Well, there were two reasons. The main reason was there wasn't enough moisture to support a cotton stalk every two or three inches, and also the soil just wasn't fertile enough to support that many healthy plants.

When we chopped to the other end of the row and back we could get a drink of water. Drinking water was taken to the field fresh twice each day. Mother would take a gallon bottle and wrap it with a burlap sack called a tow sack. The tow sack was held on to the bottle by wrapping a string around it many times until the sack was tied securely around the water bottle.

I would put a tray of ice cubes in the bottle and fill it with water. Then I let water run over the outside on the tow sack until it became soaked. Between the ice and the cooling from evaporation, the water in the bottle would remain cool for almost half a day. The bottle was refilled each half day all summer long, whether you were working on the ground chopping or picking cotton, or driving a tractor. It was a pretty good thermos. Refilling the ice trays was important if you wanted cold water that afternoon. What about the icemaker, you ask? I'm afraid there was no such thing.

The hired help (we called them hands) liked to show up about 5:00 in the morning and get started on their ten-hour day of chopping cotton before it got hot. They would take a half hour break for lunch and finish their ten-hour day about 3:30 in the afternoon. That reduced the amount of time they had to work in the hottest part of the day.

Starting to work at 5:00 AM was bad enough, but to make things worse, Dad told me that no hired help was going to chop faster that the boss's son, so I had to lead. Now I was only 13 and those 35 year-old adults could chop circles around me with one hand tied behind their back and they all knew it. But like Dad said, just because they could, did not mean they would.

There was a term the farmers used for the hands that would stop chopping and stand talking to their friends while they waited for the other choppers to catch up. It was called "leaning on the hoe" because whenever anyone stopped working and stood there in that soft dirt they would always brace themselves against the hoe in a three-point stance. Talking was not discouraged but there was always someone that was a little behind that needed to catch up.

In order to keep the group all within easy talking range, anyone could help the one behind by chopping some of their row. Any "boss man" would discourage the cotton choppers from just standing there leaning on their hoes. Even though I was young, it was also part of my job to report to Dad if the people were leaning on their hoes too much.

Anyway, when I was 14 we had a group that was working very slowly one afternoon and I told them to quit leaning on their hoes and to get back to work. That crew went back to town that night furious at being told what to do by a kid and they quit. The next day, when Dad went to hire another crew, all of the farm workers in town were talking about me. When Dad got home I think he was prouder of me than at any other time in my life. He loved the fact that the new crew knew that when I told them to get back to work I had my Dad's support. But I knew that if I wanted it to work, I might not want to overuse my newfound authority.

Another time when I was about 15, the cows had been grazing in the big cornfield eating remains from the corn harvest. Dad told me to drive the cows back into the pasture. Just in case I might be able to catch Sally, our pony, back in the far corner of our land, I took the bridle along. I did in fact manage to catch her, which was unusual. She was very hard to catch in an open field. I got aboard and was herding the cows toward the pasture when one cow tried to escape.

Sally had been trained by someone to be a cow pony, so she cut sharply to keep the cow from getting away. I did not have a saddle and the next thing I knew I was hanging upside down under the neck of a panicking pony that was running at a full gallop. Clearly I was a short timer, and not wanting to fall under her hooves, I threw myself off Sally as far sideways as I could. As I landed on my backside her hoof kicked my instep. I was limping as I finished driving the cows up on foot and then caught Sally and recovered the bridle. It took the foot a few days to quit hurting but otherwise everything was ok. I wonder if it was the same foot that I broke the little toe on when I was one?

When I was pretty small, Dad selected a healthy young heifer and gave her to me. He also opened a checking account at the bank in my name. He did this for both of my brothers, too. The heifer grew up and became a cow and since there was a bull in the pasture she began to produce calves. When the calves reached the right age they would be sold and I would get the money from my calf to save for college. Almost all of the money I earned working on the farm went into my college savings account, too.

My cow was a Jersey and produced good milk so we also used her as one of our milk cows following the birth of each of her calves. I never named my cow because she wasn't a pet. Someday she would probably be food for somebody and I understood that.

When I was in high school I started writing small checks for cash, like $10, on my account. I am pretty sure the banker told my Dad but he never mentioned it. Wow, that was freedom! Today I find it strange that the small town bank did not pay interest on the money in my account. But that was another time and place.

When we picked cotton, Dad hauled the cotton to the cotton gin, brought ice and water to the field, and took care of details like that while Mother ran the scales in the cotton patch. Anyone that drove by the cotton patch and saw people in the field could stop and ask for a job. The answer was always yes if they had their own pick sack.

First Mom would weigh their empty sack. For an adult, a cotton sack weighed 3 or 4 pounds and you only wanted to pay them for what was in the sack, but not for the weight of the sack, each time they emptied it. The trailer was in the middle of the field and cotton pickers wore kneepads. Pickers spent most of the day on their knees picking cotton and putting it, one handful at a time, into a cotton sack that was about 6 feet long. Adults would usually pick two rows at a time. They would pick from the trailer to the end of the row and turn around and pick back to the trailer. When they got back to the trailer they might be pulling as much as 50 pounds in their sack.

Then they would weigh and empty their sacks in the trailer. Mother kept a ledger on the amount of cotton each person picked. She would also look into the trailer once in a while to make sure they didn't have dirt or rocks in their pick sacks. Yes, we provided a barrel of ice water for "the white workers" and another barrel of ice water for "the other races." Each barrel had a dipper, so you would fill the dipper and drink heartily. Cotton picking was in August when temperatures frequently reached 100 degrees so it was definitely hard, hot work. When you stood and bent over to pick, instead of crawling, your back would hurt like crazy in just a few minutes.

Later, when cotton gins got more sophisticated, we quit picking the cotton out of the boll and pulled the entire cotton boll, husk and all, and put it into the sack a handful at a time. This was called pulling cotton (instead of picking it). The cotton gin would get the trash out and separate the cotton from the cottonseed (cotton seed was a separate product). The pay for pulling cotton wasn't very good. A strong adult male, working like a dog, could pull close to 600 pounds per day and I believe the pay was 60 cents a hundred in 1955.

Everybody older than about 5 had a sack and helped with the picking. The little ones would take a nap under the cotton trailer. It took a little over 2000 pounds of pulled cotton for the cotton gin to turn into a 500-pound cotton bale. Pulling cotton was only used for a few years before cotton stripper machines and cotton picking machines took the place of manual workers. I remember pulling 300 pounds in one day at the age of 13.

Dad bought a newfangled cotton stripper that winter and I never picked cotton again.

I didn't object to not having to pick cotton anymore, but then my job was to ride in the trailer behind the cotton stripper. After the cotton was stripped, it was pulled up an elevator and blown into the trailer. In order to fill the back end of the trailer someone had to use a pitchfork to throw the cotton into the back corners. One had to be careful to try and find an upwind side of the elevator to work from because there was a lot of dust and trash that would cover you up if you got downwind. It is easy to imagine how dirty I was by the end of the day after I stood sweating in that billowing dust all day.

Do you think I could have been a Dallas Cowboy if I had just hauled hay? Probably not, remember the broken toe.

Dad's Country Judgment: He doesn't have enough sense to come in out of the rain.

Dad with 1st load of Corn Shelled in Field
Photo - Rosebud News

History Lesson #16.
Hauling Corn Crop to Market at Age 13

Farm parents looked for opportunities to give their children meaningful jobs to do. At a young age we started with simple chores, which grew more complex as we grew older. When I was a child, a farmer used a planter mounted on a tractor to plant seed and cover the seed with freshly plowed dirt. One problem was the loose dirt covering the seed would quickly dry out and not leave enough moisture for the seed to germinate. So to retain the moisture, the dirt needed to be compacted, like you would if you planted seed in your flowerbed and patted it down with your hand.

But it wasn't that simple. If you compacted the dirt immediately after the planter covered the seed, the surface dirt was so damp that it would stick to the compacting wheel and actually dig up the seed you were trying to plant. So we waited a couple of hours, or overnight, before we compacted the soil covering the newly planted seed by "rolling" it.

We kept two mules and used them to pull the rollers. Robert would harness my mule, Jennie, and hook her up to a two-row roller and then he would do the same for his mule, Brownie, who would pull the four-row roller. I was about six, so we would always work in the same field and Dad threatened us both with our lives if he caught us racing the mules. We may not have actually raced them but we may have encouraged them with a few "Giddy Ups" once in a while. I'm quite sure those mules were very obedient to the stern commands from a 6 year old and an 11 year old kid.

Dad said if I ever had a problem controlling my mule I was to turn around and just hop off the back of the roller since the mules could not easily back up while hitched to the roller. One day one of the reins on Jennie's bridle came lose and I had no way to control her. So just like Dad had told me, I turned around and hopped off the back. When Jennie got to the end of the row she stopped and waited for directions on which way to turn. Robert came over and reattached the rein so I could continue. Those mules knew more about farming than I probably ever did.

Until the time I was about 8, ripe corn was harvested by physically yanking the ears from the cornstalk and throwing them into a pile to be picked up later. This is the way it had always been done. Corn stalks are taller than the workers so there would be no air circulation in the middle of a corn patch in late July. This would be very hot, physical work. I was not strong enough to pull the ear of corn off of the stalk when I was that young.

Once the corn had been placed in piles I would go along to the field with two workers. One of them would be my dad. My job was to drive the mules, which were pulling a trailer, up to the piles of corn. The two grown ups would toss the ears of corn from that pile into a washtub and dump the tub into the trailer. I would then pull up to the next pile of corn and they would repeat putting the corn in the washtub and dumping it into the trailer. By the time I was 10, a small tractor had replaced Jennie and Brownie. Like I said, everything was changing very quickly and it cost too much to feed the mules if you weren't going to use them more than three or four weeks a year.

One learns to drive at a young age on the farm. It starts with small tractors and just sort of builds from there. Dad had a two-row corn-picking machine by the time I was in junior high. When I was 13, Robert was out of high school and working at the cotton gin in town, so it was going to be my job to haul the corn crop to town to be sold. I could not get a driver's license until I was 14 but it was legal for youngsters under 14 to drive a tractor on the public road.

So Dad decided I would use a tractor to pull trailer loads of corn to town. We had a large tractor that would run about 20 miles an hour but at that speed I wouldn't be able to haul the crop to the granary on the far side of town as quickly as the corn picker could gather it. Dad decided I would be able to keep up if he hooked two trailers together. A route through town was selected and a notch on the tractor throttle was marked for the speed I was to drive.

All went well and everybody in Rosebud got used to seeing me come through town back and forth on those back streets about four round trips a day. Of course, I felt like pretty big stuff whenever I saw a school friend from my perch high up on that big tractor.

Since the trailers were only used for about 6 weeks per years, the tires seldom wore out. However, they would eventually rot and it was not unusual to have a flat tire on those rocky gravel roads. There was a jack in the tractor's toolbox and I threw a spare tire in each trailer after it was filled with corn. I would usually have about three flat tires a week and with a little practice, I got to where I could change a flat in about 10 minutes. I would take the flat tire to Huddleson's Humble gas station where my high school friend Jackie worked and he would fix the flat. When the tires were no longer repairable Dad would buy used tires to replace them because they would rot before they wore out anyway.

One day near the end of the harvest during my 13th year (note: my birthday was in May so I was just barely 13), I was pulling two trailers loaded with corn to town with the tractor. The county maintainers (us country folks call it a road grader) had graded out the ditches for better drainage.

The gravel roads had one set of tracks down the middle with loose gravel on both sides and I pulled into the gravel to meet a car coming toward me. The first trailer "whipped" a little in the loose gravel and the second trailer skidded into the steeply graded ditch and turned over. At that moment I discovered I could really stop quickly. At least it was ear corn and not shelled corn. I used my cell phone to call home—wait just a minute, there wouldn't be any cell phones for another 35 or more years. I walked about a half mile to the nearest house and got the neighbor to call home.

Mother got Dad out of the field and he came and got me. We returned home and got a big chain and an elevator with a gasoline motor. First we used the tractor and the chain to pull the trailer back upright. Then it probably took the two of us less than an hour, using the elevator, to reload the corn on the trailer.

What is an elevator you ask? An elevator is kind of like a mini escalator only it is used to lift something like corn up a narrow chute (about one foot wide) and dump it when it gets to the top. It has many uses but the most common is to aid getting ear corn up to an opening high on the side of the barn. Farmers always kept some of the corn they harvested in a corncrib (which is just a room in the barn where corn is stored) for their own use. Without the elevator you had to pitch it up high through the opening one shovel full at a time. It was backbreaking work. So we stuck the top end of the elevator through the window in the barn. Then we backed the trailer up to the bottom end of the elevator and just pushed the corn out the back of the trailer. It would fall into the elevator, which would pull it up and dump it into the corncrib.

Obviously another use for an elevator could be to reload a trailer that an innocent child had turned over. I do recall that Dad was a bit irritated that he was unable to finish the field he was harvesting until the next day. Otherwise it wasn't a real big deal. I mean how fast could I have been going if the tractor didn't go but 20 miles an hour wide open. I will admit (now) that it never occurred to me to let off on the throttle—even when I pulled into the loose gravel to meet that car. But there were some things Dad didn't need to know.

One reason it probably wasn't a bigger deal was that not long before my accident, Dad had been pulling a trailer of corn down the road behind a tractor. When he drove through a low place in the road the pin that hooked the trailer to the tractor was kicked out by the gravel road and the trailer ran off the road, turning over. "Like father, like son."

We raised a lot of corn and once I was 14, I got my driver's license and could haul the corn to town using our pickup to pull a trailer. Now I could drive faster than 20 miles per hour. I still remember driving a little fast over a rough bridge one day and snapping off the huge bolt on the trailer frame, called the kingpin. The front tires of the trailer pivoted around the king pin, which allowed the trailer to turn corners.

The entire load fell on the front two trailer tires and I came to another rather sudden stop right in the middle of that bridge. With practice, I was getting better and better at stopping really quickly. Remember the procedure where the state trooper asked you to jam on your brakes and stop quickly when you took your driver's license test? Well there I was out there all by myself developing all of these new ways to stop quickly.

Soon after I got into high school, Dad decided he could make more money from his grain crop if he got a big self propelled combine that could harvest and shell the corn in the field. Here is why. Corn was sold by the bushel. 96 pounds of corn on the cob was a bushel. 56 pounds of shelled corn was a bushel. Dad figured out that the hybrid corn he grew took less than 90 pounds, maybe only 85 pounds, to make a 56 pound bushel of shelled corn.

The people that bought the corn at the granary paid him a little extra per bushel for the shelled corn because they did not have to shell it. (A few years ago my sister-in-law Sharon gave me the picture in front of this chapter from the Rosebud News of Dad delivering the first load of corn that had ever been shelled in the field and delivered to Zipperlen's Rosebud Feed and Grain.)

Dad constructed a really well built trailer to haul the shelled corn to town. He built it tight so it would not leak the corn kernels and strong so it would handle a heavy load. And it had dual wheels on the back axle. Just a note about building a trailer—when you wanted to build a trailer you went to a junkyard and brought the frame of an old car or pickup truck. No cab or engine or gas tank or stuff like that—just the frame, wheels and tires. The trailer was built on the car frame (or in this case—the heavy duty pickup frame with dualies) and a tongue was welded to the front axle so you could hook the trailer behind a tractor or pickup and pull it.

The sideboards were bolted to 2 by 4 vertical studs. Dad would borrow an electric drill from the cotton ginner, Clarence Wolf, and drill holes through the trailer sideboards and the vertical 2 by 4 studs. Somebody had to stick the bolts through the holes that Dad drilled and then put on a washer and tighten the nuts on the bolts. I filled the role of that somebody quite well. Of course a young boy could always help paint a trailer because no one cared if the job wasn't perfect or if you dripped a little paint on the ground. Dad or Robert would come along behind me and touch up any mess I made anyway. But that was done on pretty days in the wintertime, under that oak shade tree with the tree house in it, so it was more fun than work.

The loaded pickup and trailer grossed out at about 14,000 pounds when both were loaded with shelled corn and it seemed as if it took about a quarter of a mile to stop, especially in loose gravel. I wouldn't have been able to stop that quickly if Dad hadn't filled the back end of the pickup with shelled corn so the pickup tires could get some traction.

There was a spot where the gravel road T'ed into a paved Farm To Market road about two miles from town. Of course there was a stop sign there. I had to start stopping well before I got to that intersection and even then the trailer would try to push the entire load right past that stop sign. In reality I never quite stopped. Once I had slowed down to a couple of miles an hour and it was clear that I could stop if a car was coming (and there wasn't a cop anywhere around) I would slam it into first gear and hit the gas because it was hard to get that sucker moving if I ever came to a complete stop.

A couple of years later Dad bought a bob tailed truck (a one piece truck without a separate trailer—it had 10 wheels, not 18, and the bed had a hydraulic lift). By now I was about 17 and the truck loaded with corn probably grossed out at about 33,000 pounds. But it was much easier to get the truck rolling and also to stop than the pickup had been. Dad decided he could get a better price at the granary in Cameron that year, which was another 17 miles further, so I had to haul that crop through Rosebud to Cameron. At least the extra miles were on a paved highway. Once I got to Cameron I could dump the load really quickly with the hydraulic lift.

On one of the early trips that summer I noticed in the side rear view mirrors that a lot of grain was blowing out the back of the truck at highway speeds. Then when I got to the granary in Cameron I checked the bed of the truck and it was obvious I had lost some grain. When I told Dad about it he said not to worry, but I did. After that I went into the tractor shed and got the big heavy tarpaulin and from then on when the truck was loaded I covered the corn with the tarp and tied it down tightly before I left the field. I was proud of the money I saved for my Dad that harvest.

By then I was probably driving 55 miles per hour and the people I met on US 77 that summer had no idea how lucky they were that their lives were being spared—on a road with a kid driving a truck—yet one more day. In case you're wondering, a farm boy did not require a commercial license to drive his dad's farm truck.

Whenever I did not have a load of corn to drive to town, I was to shred corn stalks with the shredder pulled by our small Farmall C tractor. One day the truck was parked in the middle of a 150-acre field where I was shredding harvested corn stalks. It was late and time to quit for the day. At the end of the row I pulled the tractor up behind the truck and got off the tractor and into the truck so I could drive it to the house.

Since the truck bed is behind the cab there is no rear view mirror in the middle of the windshield, only mirrors on each side of the truck. Earlier I had decided that I would always get out of the truck and look behind me before backing up just to be sure I never backed into anything. I started to get out of the truck to look behind me and then I thought, "What could be behind me? I am in the middle of a 150-acre field?" So I started the truck, threw it in reverse and backed into that Farmall C. Oops!

Well Dad spent a little money doing minimal repairs on the tractor. The front end was a little crumpled but he got it running again. About a week later I drove that same tractor pulling the same shredder to the house for lunch. The truck was already loaded with corn and parked beside the road in the front yard waiting for me to drive it to town. I parked the tractor behind it and went into the house to eat with the family.

When I finished eating I came out of the house and walked between the tractor and the truck and got into the truck. I needed to turn the truck around so I could head the other way, so I started the engine, put it in reverse and backed into that same tractor again. I never said I was perfect. I mean, I just backed that same truck into that same tractor two teensy weensy times.

I have one more story about Dad and his combine I want to tell. Dad had just achieved a major life accomplishment (he didn't call it that but we all understood that it was, anyway) and bought his first self-propelled combine that could harvest grain and pick and shell corn in the field. He was one proud farmer! He finished harvesting our maize crop that first year but had a couple of weeks before he would start gathering his own corn so he was combining maize for a neighboring farmer.

It was summer time and I was there helping position the truck and making myself useful doing any thing he might need done. It was closing in on 10:00 at night when Dad decided to shut it down for the day and go home and get some sleep. We came back the next morning and the first thing Dad saw in the bright light of day was a concrete pillar nestled between the maize stalks in the very next row he would combine. It was some kind of a county survey marker the landowner had failed to point out to Dad. If Dad had made one more round the night before, he would have run it up into his prized new combine and done a huge amount of damage. Whew! He never said so but I bet he was almost ill when he saw that concrete post.

> Country Boy on Regulators: Enron talked the SEC officials into allowing Enron to redefine how their profits were calculated. The SEC officials, who allowed these deviations from standard accounting practices, should serve jail time just like those people from Enron, maybe longer. And I have never heard of even one SEC official suffering any repercussions for their part in this business travesty.

Two Row Roller

History Lesson #17.
Witching for Water

We had several sources of water on the farm but our main source was a water well that had very good water. When I was about six we had an underground gasoline tank installed next to the driveway that was only used for tractors, of course, because we hadn't paid the gasoline road tax. Even though the underground storage tank was new it had a fault and a couple of years later it sprang a leak. It just so happened that the underground spring that fed the water well ran directly from the storage tank to the well, and we had to abandon our wonderful well.

Dad had a friend come out from Rosebud and witch for water to try and find a location for a new well. He turned a Y shaped limb he had cut from a tree (I don't know what kind of tree) upside down and held one end of the fork of the Y in each hand. When he got over a location that had underground water the limb that was pointed up would bend over and point at the ground. There was a lot of tension in the stick so it flexed quite a bit as it gradually bent until it pointed down.

He marked about a dozen potential points were we might drill for water. Dad and I watched the entire process and I still find it hard to believe what I saw. We drilled at most of the sites and hit at least some water at every spot he marked. We took the best of the bunch and dug a new well but the water was never as good as that first well and after that we installed a cistern next to the house and used that for drinking water.

A cistern is a large round tin container that is used to collect and store rainwater. It is placed next to a building that has gutters to channel the rain that runs off the roof, into the cistern. A good rain would fill a cistern in only a couple of hours. Depending on its size, a cistern might hold enough water to supply all of the water needed by a cautious household for four to six months even without another rain.

If it was installed on an elevated platform, it worked like a single-family water tower with gravity flow providing water pressure. This was the only way to have running water throughout a house before farms had electricity to run a pump.

After our well went bad, Dad bought a second very large cistern that was as tall as the two-story barn and about 15 feet across. He had it installed next to the barn to provide water for the livestock and do things like flush the toilets and wash clothes but we did not use it for our drinking water.

When I was about 13 Dad noticed the water from that cistern suddenly smelled bad. The screen over the in-spout had accidentally moved and a few rats had gotten in the cistern and drowned. Dad drained the cistern but it still had about 3 inches of water in the bottom. Early one morning I was sent down into the cistern to remove the dead rats and the last bit of water. Of course, it was in the summer and quite hot in the bottom of that cistern.

I would fill a bucket with water and silt off the bottom and Dad would pull it to the top with a rope and dump it out over the side. Man that was a nasty job! But it only lasted two hours so it was just another interesting farm boy experience.

You would think we would have had to mop it dry and really clean the walls and bottom of that cistern, but we did not even come close. After we got the decaying rats out (as well as possible) we probably emptied the cistern down to about an inch of water and silt. Then I think Dad got bored and he decided we had cleaned it well enough because it would get thoroughly diluted when it filled up after the next rain. Life on the farm is a little different from life in the city. Or maybe it's not that different but we just don't know it.

Even though the town's motto was "Everything is Rosy in Rosebud," just like any other place, it wasn't always quite that idyllic. I suspect some of you have been given a speeding ticket in Rosebud because they had a speed trap there for quite a few years after I left town. I remember returning to visit my parents one night and getting pulled over by the local police on Main Street for speeding. He told me I was the third Skupin boy he had stopped, however, I think it was the one time in my life where I actually talked my way out of a ticket.

You may think that one of the good things about living in a small town is that you don't have to worry about dirty politics. Remember gerrymandering? It is rigging the voting boundaries to get the election results you want. One year when I was in high school the city of Rosebud desperately needed another source for water. The problem was that the local leaders came up with a plan to create a Pond Creek Watershed by building lakes on about a dozen of the larger gullies that fed Pond Creek.

The farmers, who had created their own water supplies (especially those who didn't even have land that bordered the creek), opposed the plan because they would be paying the majority of the cost for supplying water for the town. An election was to be held and in general it was pretty obvious who supported the Watershed and who opposed it. When the local politicians drew the boundaries for who could vote, the voting boundary would come down a county road and then jog around the house of anyone that opposed the watershed.

The Wimberly property boundary ran along a straight county road. But I saw a map where the voting boundaries were drawn along the road until it came to their house. Then it turned to exclude their house and barn from the voting area before returning to the road. Of course, 99% of the Wimberly land would still be in the watershed, so the Wimberlys would still be fully taxed, but they would not be allowed to vote since there house was not in the watershed boundaries.

The election passed but the farmers continued to protest the results on the grounds that the voting boundaries were illegal. One day six of the farmers went to Austin to see their state representatives to protest the election. Dad was one of them. They drove around the capital several times but could not find a parking space. Finally they found a very small space they could pull the nose of the car into. Then they all got out and lifted the back end of the car into the tight parking space.

It took a lot of hard work to kill the beast that was the Pond Creek Watershed but the farmers knew they were right and they were eventually able to get the courts to agree that the politicians from Rosebud had gerrymandered the voting boundaries and the water project was overturned.

Country Boy observation: Whenever your boss gives you a job to do look for ways to do more than what was requested. After you finish, discreetly take credit and point out to your boss what you have done. Doing more than is expected of you will help you get ahead in life.

Skupin Boys
Henry, David and Robert

History Lesson #18.
Even in the Land of Milk and Honey

Yes, even in the land of milk and honey there are teenagers. Every once in a while they do a few things they aren't supposed to do and a few they may not ever tell their parents. Well, the boys do anyway. I'm not sure about the girls. Who knows, there may be a few stories about me that won't appear in this book, even 47 years after high school.

I remember one night when about half the football team had the flu and our coach had to cancel the Friday night game. We usually only played about 13 or 14 players the whole game so we just couldn't field a team with so many players sick. The last thing the coach told us Friday afternoon before we left school was to go home and get some sleep. He didn't want us going out to another Friday night football game and getting sick because it was very cold that day.

So naturally Marvin Spivey and I went to the high school game in Marlin and we just about froze to death. I still remember going to the Dairy King a few blocks from the stadium after the game. I bought hot chocolate and I was still so cold that I was shaking and spilt the hot chocolate all over my lap. But just in case you are wondering, neither Marvin nor I got sick. And I don't remember us talking with the coach about the game in Marlin either.

One year Halloween fell on Thursday night and the last thing the coach told us after football practice that day was to go home and get some sleep. He didn't want us running around "trick or treating" and getting into trouble. Well, a cousin of mine, Marvin Bernsen, had a Model A Ford Coupe we all liked to ride on. Only two people could get inside, but we could ride on the front fenders, stand on the running boards, or even stand on the back bumper. Practically the whole football team was hanging onto Marvin's Model A riding around Rosebud that Halloween night.

Later we stopped at Swanzy's Dairy King and were standing around talking when the starting center, Robert Ocker, walked up. His clothes were all torn and he was *skint* (skinned) up from head to toe. Seems Robert had been standing on the back bumper and there wasn't much to hold on to back there. When Marvin had turned a corner, Robert had fallen off but no one noticed he was gone. I don't remember if Robert played that Friday night or not. If he did I'm sure he was well aware of that mishap during the game.

At Halloween the shenanigans tended to get a little out of hand in small towns back in those days. The words were trick or treat. But that included quite a bit more "trick" than treat. The boys would roam town in carloads and throw eggs at each other. Of course the eggs seldom hit the other boys, they usually just hit the cars. Dad did complain the next morning when the pickup was all sticky from being hit by about a hundred eggs the night before.

I do remember all of the cars just happened to stop at the same time near the high school one Halloween evening. Right next to the road that ran by the front of the school was a telephone pole. It was just lying there. The telephone company had placed it there to install it the next day. "Temptation!" Well, all of the boys got together and picked up the telephone pole, carried it about 40 yards, and placed it across the wide concrete banisters, thereby blocking the stairs that led into the front of the high school.

Then the boys in all of the other cars decided to chunk eggs at the kids in the back of our pickup. I was busy rolling up the driver's side window while the boys in the back of the pickup were getting plastered with eggs. After about two seconds I finally got my window rolled up and then started the pickup and we got out of there.

My friends thought I could have driven away a bit quicker but they were missing an important point. I didn't get hit with a single egg. The main target of Halloween mischief was always the high school. Robert reports they took apart a walking cultivator and reassembled it on the 3rd floor on the high school stage one year. I'm glad my class didn't do bad stuff like that. Where were the girls, you ask? Oh, they were around.

The Swanzy's Dairy King was owned and operated by Eddie's parents and when I spent the night with Eddie he would go in and make us hamburgers and milk shakes just like he owned the place. Another thing different back in those days is that there were no fast food places in the 40's and 50's. Of course a lot of people sold hamburgers. But when you ordered a hamburger they put a piece of raw hamburger meat on the grill and started preparing your burger. It wasn't particularly fast.

No fried chicken places with ready-to-serve chicken, no Burger King or McDonalds, no pizza places to speak of (when you did find a place with pizzas you had to wait forever), no taco places and almost the only place where you could even eat out for breakfast was a grill, and that wasn't fast food either. Drive through any area of town today with all of those fast food restaurants and take a look around. None of those companies even existed that short time ago.

I think all three of the Skupin boys may have driven a wee bit faster than we should have from time to time. One day when Robert was in high school he took off very fast and went to speed shift from 1st to 2nd gear. When he jammed it into second gear it went into reverse instead and stripped the gears. I think the car would only go into 3rd gear so he had to limp home that way and tell Dad what he had done.

During Robert's senior year in high school he wanted a stereo but didn't have the money to buy one. He found an old jukebox that was being discarded and made his own. He removed the amplifiers and speakers and built separate boxes for each of them and wired everything together. His scavenged stereo worked pretty well and he was happy with that solution for a couple of years. But as soon as he could scrape enough money together he bought a mail order do-it-yourself kit and used his soldering iron to build himself a brand new amplifier.

We kids were quick to take advantage of the Germans and Czechs attitude about teenagers and beer. Teenagers would all go to the SPJST Halls on Friday or Saturday night. We always said you could buy a beer at most

SPJST Halls if you were tall enough to put your money on the bar. In the few cases where they wouldn't sell it to us directly we could always find a friendly adult to make sure we got what we wanted.

The bands were mostly Czech polka bands and they played lots of polkas and waltzes. Entire Czech and German families came to the dances, grandparents, parents, and even small children. Early in the evening the children would get out on the dance floor and imitate their parents. Later, when they got tired I would see them over in a corner asleep on two chairs pulled together or even sprawled out on the wooden floor. It was also common for a small child to be asleep on a quilt on top of a table while the music and the dancing swirled around them.

I have always been somewhat naïve but as far as I know illegal drugs just weren't a problem back before the Vietnam War. I knew of the words cocaine, heroin, and marijuana, but the main problems we faced were beer, liquor, and maybe smoking. Kids were discouraged from smoking by most adults, but since it was not considered a health risk, nor was it illegal, and smoking was portrayed as cool by Hollywood, many kids became smokers in high school.

In the 1960's, with better transportation, more money and a backlash against authority and the government, illegal drugs quickly became a major problem even in backwater places like Rosebud. I think the Vietnam war probably was a big factor in the surge of drugs problems that face the world today.

Like many places, Rosebud had a Veterans of Foreign Wars Hall. Our VFW Hall had two pool tables and one of them was reserved for teenagers. Even in exciting places like Rosebud a teenager can sometimes find himself with little to do. We would just go down to the VFW Hall, get Bill Johnson (he wasn't very young but he took good care of us kids) to rack-em, And we would shoot a few games of pool. Mom wasn't all that comfortable with me going to a place where the members came in and drank beer but it did keep me off the streets and out of trouble so she never said not to go.

By the time I reached the 9th grade I was 6 feet tall and a lean 119-pound teenager. Surely I would be a good athlete now because I offered little wind resistance when I ran. Still, no matter how much I tried I never ran very fast—and I was a pretty mediocre pool shooter too. Probably that broken little toe when I was one-year-old, don't you think?

Once I was in high school I usually went to town on Saturday night. Sometime I would have a date, more so after I got to be about 16. Other times I would just do stuff with my friends, like Marvin Spivey and Jackie McCollum. By about 10:30 we would start arriving back to town from movies or whatever we had been doing and we would meet up at the Texaco station by the blinking red light (it was closed by that time of night.)

Donald Thweatt, the city policeman, would be there to write tickets for anyone who ran the stoplight and he would be included in the bull sessions we held next to the gas pumps. When four to six of us showed up we would all pile into a car and drive 17 miles over to the Texan Restaurant in Cameron which never closed. By the time we got there we would be giddy and laugh at just about anything anyone said. Even though we would be loud, I don't ever remember them asking us to hold the noise down. Everyone would get either a chicken fried steak or a hamburger steak and we would swap stories for about an hour and then we would return to Rosebud and go home.

Rosebud High did not offer an extremely broad set of courses so I took FFA (Future Farmers of America) to fill out my class schedule. FFA required each student to do a shop project each year. As a freshman I made a shoe shine kit with a place on top where I could put my foot while I shined my shoe. I still have that shoe shine kit. As a sophomore I made a bookcase for our new bedroom but I used lumber that was a little too cheap and the boards warped so I wasn't very pleased with the finished project that year.

Dad had a trailer that he wanted to rebuild with a wider bed. (The floor of the trailer was called the bed.) It was important that the bed be centered over the frame of the trailer. Otherwise the trailer would not track (follow behind) the pickup in a straight line. I built the trailer bed my junior year and was quite proud of that school project. One thing that made the projects harder was that our teacher, Mr. Jackson, would not let us use power tools because he thought we needed to learn the basics.

One day Mr. Jackson took the FFA class on a field trip to castrate some young calves for a farmer that lived near town. Once a young male calf is castrated it is referred to as a steer. A steer will put on weight faster than a young bull and the meat will be more tender so almost all young male calves are turned into steers. I had helped Dad do this job many times, as had the other farm boys in the class, so this wasn't really anything new to us.

But something went wrong that day and when we finished with one of the calves it had gone into shock and died. So Mr. Jackson took his knife and cut the calf's throat to drain its blood. Then we got a trailer so the animal could be hauled to the Kirkscey Locker Plant in town and butchered for its meat. I never did know this particular farmer and he wasn't even there that day, but I am sure that was one embarrassing field trip for Mr. Jackson.

Another off campus event that took place was summer camp on Lake Marble Falls for the FFA boys. Camp was a five-day four-night event and Mr. Jackson would get two parents with fishing boats to come along for the week of adventure. The boats would go out and run their trout lines early in the morning and again late in the afternoon. We would each draw kitchen duty about twice per camp and I think the main thing we did was goof off.

We were playing poker for matchsticks one year when a friend of Mr. Jackson threw $20 in the pot and said, "Lets all play for that." He then proceeded to win it all back, one hand at a time. They were our cards but it seemed as if he knew every card we held and it was a good lesson in gambling for us kids. Everybody tried smoking at summer camp but I don't think many of us took it up later.

The Rosebud FFA (as in Future Farmers of America—just for boys) and FHA (as in Future Homemakers of America—just for girls) each took a bus to the State Fair of Texas every year. It was always on the Texas—OU football weekend. The fair grounds would be packed. Maybe they didn't want the boys and girls to ride together for some reason or other, but I can't imagine what that would be.

When I was a senior my friend David McAtee worked out a plan. After the out-of-town Friday night football game in Rogers, five us went over to his house and spent the night. It was a very short night because I think we got to bed about 1:00 and then got up about 4:30 so we could follow the two Rosebud buses to Dallas. We were a little tired because we had all played at least 75% of both offense and defense in the game the night before. (We didn't have a lot of players and only played about 14 guys the entire game.)

At the fair we each bought a little black hat with a pink feather up the side and our name in pink letters on the bill. And to make us the coolest six boys who ever went to the State Fair, we were in David's new baby blue Chevrolet convertible—with the top down, of course.

The day was fantastic but all good things must come to an end, so we finally headed for home about 5:00 that evening. Somehow we got turned around and found ourselves heading towards Corsicana instead of Waco. No big problem, really. Just go out to the edge of Dallas and hook a right over to the next highway, which ran to Waco.

But we did have a problem. This school bus full of really good looking FHA girls managed to get right in front of our windshield. And we seemed to bypass every opportunity to hook that right and get back over to US 77. Well, would you believe it, that darn bus got about 30 miles out of Dallas and turned left, instead of right, and David's Chevy just followed it.

About an hour later we all found ourselves in the house of one of the blonds along with several of her friends. Must have taken us a good three hours to get that Chevy restarted and turned around headed for home. I do remember that about 10 miles from home the driver (it may have been Marvin by this time) dozed off and the only person still awake was Billy Pattillo in the back right seat. He had time to lean forward quickly and wake the driver up (along with everybody else) when the car hit the shoulder. It was tough for me to stay awake all alone on that six-mile drive from town to the farm when we finally got back to Rosebud.

Rosebud High did one thing that I thought was very helpful in preparing the graduates for life after high school. We had a 30 minute period every school day in the spring semester when all of the students were required to take part in an academic University Inter-Scholastic League (UIL) event. Some of the kids did not play sports, they weren't in the band or pep squad, they just went to class. Given a choice some of these students would choose not to participate in any extra curricular events.

Texas has a statewide competition in many academic events much like the competition for the State Championship in Football. Some of the events were number sense, debate, one act play, declamation, poetry reading, spelling, extemporaneous speaking, essay writing, typing, slide rule (replaced by calculator today), accounting (added since I was in high school), drafting, etc. In addition, UIL (in the spring semester) also included outdoor sports such as track, volleyball, softball and events like that.

Rosebud was always by far the smallest school in the district but we were usually first or second in district in UIL. We all learned a skill or two from competing that served us well in life. Anton Zucha didn't take part in many school activities, but at a recent reunion he pointed out that he was on the debate team with Delores Wunsch. Delores was the head cheerleader. Dumb me. I was doing slide rule and number sense with a bunch of boys.

Today the Rosebud Accounting team has won just about every UIL meet they have ever competed in, including all their practice meets—some of which were against large Houston schools. When I say all meets, I mean ALL meets. They have won the state championship every single year for about the last 14 years. Coach Barkemeyer must be some teacher/coach! A few years ago the Rosebud all-state quarterback was on the accounting team. They don't just beat the opponents—they crush them!

I played football on the same field with some pretty good athletes at one time or another. Some local boys and several guys we played against were really outstanding. Quite a few of the Rosebud athletes earned scholarships and played very well in college. But I think the best football player I was ever on the field with was Alton McNew. I still remember scrimmaging against him in the 8th grade. He ran straight over the top of me one time. One foot landed by my left hip and the other just right of my head. Coach Hoelscher got a big laugh out of that.

Alton left Rosebud after his freshman year when his Dad got a job in Waco. He was high school All-American at Waco University High and went to Baylor where he was a star on the freshman team. Unfortunately, following the death of his parents in a traffic accident, he had to drop out of college to help raise his younger sisters. Years later I was passing through Waco and stopped to buy gasoline at a service station. Alton pulled in driving a gravel truck. We only got to talk for a few minutes. Small world, isn't it!

Remember, at the beginning of this chapter when I said there were stories about me that I never told my parents and there may be a few stories about me that won't appear in this book, even 47 years after high school. Here is one of those I never told my parents. One night three of us spent the night with a friend, David Repka, so we could go jackrabbit hunting (in a pasture that we did not have permission to enter). We all had shotguns. Two boys would ride in the back of our pickup and the driver (me) would chase the jackrabbit through the pasture while the boys in the back shot at it.

We were going pretty fast and the rabbit was darting back and forth and running like crazy when one of the boys started beating on the roof of the pickup hollering for me to stop. David McAtee had lost his balance and fallen out of the back of the speeding pickup with his shotgun. I doubt if it was on safety since he was trying to shoot that jackrabbit.

We went back to get him and he said he was ok but I would bet he had a few more scratches and sore spots the next day than he admitted. Later that same evening we got our pickup stuck in a mud hole and we had to go get the rancher's tractor (which was near the pasture we were hunting in and just happened to have the key in the ignition) and pull our pickup out of the mud hole. David Repka reported the rancher wasn't very happy the next morning about the tracks the pickup left all over his pastureland and the use of his tractor. Imagine that! But boys will be boys.

> Country Boy on Politicians: I do understand that there is power in numbers. But whenever I see every congressperson voting the party line on an issue it infuriates me. Don't elected officials know we elected them to represent their constituents and to do what is best for the country rather than just be sheep?

Hay Rake

History Lesson #19.
Farming—Way Back Then

Dad was a dry land farmer, which meant the only water for the crops was from rain. No one in that area irrigated. If it did not rain when the crops needed rain, the crops for the entire year could be lost. If you got some rain, but not enough or at the wrong time, the crops might be stunted and produce poorly. We grew cotton, corn, maize, and we grew some crops that would be baled and fed to livestock, especially in the winter, such as alfalfa hay. Our cows were always as fat as any cows I saw because they were well fed. I was proud to have a "row crop farmer" for a dad.

When I was seven or eight years old Dad had a hay baler that was very primitive. It was unlike any baler I have ever seen. It had a one-cylinder gasoline engine that ran very slowly but produced a lot of power. Until about 15 years ago hay bales were about 18 inches high, 24 inches wide and 48 inches long. Two wires that were wrapped tightly, lengthwise around the bale, held each bale together. This special wire was called baling wire. First the hay was cut and allowed to lie on the ground for a few days to dry. Otherwise the moisture in the stalks would cause the baled hay to overheat and rot. Farmers really worried about getting a rain and having it ruin their hay crop while it was lying on the ground drying out before baling.

After he baled his own hay, Dad would bale other peoples' to earn a little extra money. First he would park what is now that antique hay baler in the middle of the area where hay had been cut to be baled. Three men fed the hay into the hay baler—one pitchfork at a time. A very large riding rake, almost as wide as a car is long, drug the hay up near the baler. The people with the pitchforks would put the hay into the bailer, which would compress it into a bale.

Baling wire was poked between the bales and pulled through and then poked back through on the other end of the bale. Once it was wrapped all the way around the bale an adult would tie the wire so the bale would not come open when it was spit out the back of the baler. My job, at age seven or eight, was to pull the wire through and then poke it back through on the other end of the bale so the adult could hand tie both wires around the bale.

I think the hay rake was pulled by a couple of mules and the tines on the rake worked a little like a leaf rake except each tine was about three feet long. Robert would often be the hay rake operator. It took a crew of about five or six people to bale hay. By the time I was about 9 years old that baler was obsolete and the "New Holland" baler had replaced it ("New Hol land," like "John Deere," was the name of a corporation.)

The only person needed to operate the New Holland baler was the tractor driver (unless something didn't work). It picked the hay up from the ground, made a bale out of it, tied the baling wire around it, and spit it out the back without being touched by human hands. As I have said before, "the times, they were a changing." Even the shape of the bales has changed today. Hay balers now make large round bales. Baling hay today is so different than it was then that I doubt if many people younger than about 55 have ever heard of the type of antiquated hay baler Dad had, even if they grew up on a farm.

As Dad bought more and bigger machinery he continued to hire out to work for other farmers. He would bale their hay, use his corn picker, cotton stripper, combine, and terracing equipment to bring in extra income. This was called "working for the public." But he always took care of his own crops first and only worked for the public after his own crop was gathered.

By the time my younger brother David started farming in the mid 70's the original 320-acre farm had grown to 582 acres and David rented another 100 acres or so. In 1942 it probably took more than 100 people, (including a lot of teenagers and day laborers who helped in the summertime) to farm that much land. Children could chop weeds and pick cotton. Parents were always looking for ways to let the kids contribute a little to the family income.

Dad had a few farming concepts that I don't think everyone followed at that time. First he planted his crops as early as possible after the last freeze. He had a thermometer that he would stick into the ground and as soon as the ground reached a certain temperature he started planting. If it froze again, he replanted, but it seldom did. He said crops always brought the best prices when people first started harvesting and before anyone knew how big the total nationwide crop would be for that year. South central Texas was warmer than most of the nation so if he planted earlier than other people he could harvest before prices started falling.

Also planting early gave the plants the advantage of maturing before the long hot summers peaked. I remember one time after David took over the farm when the weatherman said it was going to freeze in three days. David decided it would probably only freeze for one night and the plants would not have popped out of the ground yet. He planted like crazy for those three days so that once the freeze had passed he would already have his seed in the ground. Wow, that is aggressive farming! It worked too!

There were two times a year when Dad worked from before sunup until after sundown. One was when he planted. He wanted to get the seed into the ground quickly before a rainy spell could set in. A prolonged rainy spell might cause a farmer to make a bad crop or even keep him from ever getting it planted and thus miss an entire crop altogether. Another time when he worked especially long days was when the crop was ready to harvest.

He harvested our crops before he used his equipment to work for others. He never knew when a storm might come and wipe our crop out if it was left in the fields after it was ripe. He had already spent all of the money and time and effort to grow the crop. The income from our crop was 100% ours. So he would get after it and not stop until the crop was in.

Dad would loose about 20 pounds each summer from the hard work. Then he would gain it back over the winter when things slowed down. Every time we drove past this one farm, on the way to town, Dad would just shake his head because the farmer didn't harvest his corn until about two months after Dad was through. As Kenny Rogers almost sang, "There'll be time enough for counting when the harvesting's done."

Every farmer was looking for an edge to get ahead. For Dad the "Investment Tax Credit" was a huge help. He tried to buy a new piece of big machinery almost every year so he could use the "Investment Tax Credit" to reduce his taxes. That way he let Uncle Sam pay part of the cost of upgrading his farm equipment in the form of lower taxes. Big business used this tax break all the time. So did Dad. Even back then, he paid the extra money for a good accountant. Who'd a thunk it!

Dad had a series of farmhands who worked for him. One that made an impression on me was Frank Thompson. Frank was a graduate of the black Wilson High School in Rosebud and very athletic. The track coach took his team to the state meet in Austin and when an official asked him where his team was the coach pointed at Frank. Frank won 3 events and placed second in two others and Wilson High won the state meet that day. Robert said he worked with Frank hauling hay after Frank came to work for Dad, and that he was incredibly strong.

Back in the 40's and 50's farms were full of houses for the farm labors to live in. Our farm had three houses for the hands but two of them burned. While I was growing up, I saw six different farm house burn to the ground. Even as a small child, watching a house burn felt tragic. Once a farm building caught on fire it was probably going to burn completely down to the ground before the Rosebud volunteer fire department could get there. Since telephones weren't everywhere like today, it wasn't uncommon just not to bother calling the fire department because by the time someone got to a telephone it was already too late.

Once the one room school in Briary closed, Dad bought the teacherage and moved it to a location where one of our rent houses had burned. The new house had indoor plumbing and a cistern was placed next to the house so that it had gravity flow running water and indoor toilets. That was pretty advanced for a farm labor's house. However, less and less labor was needed to run the farms and hundreds of these houses were eventually left empty to rot.

But there is always a catch to watch out for. The county taxed the farmer for each building on the farm. So the farmers and ranchers eventually tore down the unneeded houses to avoid being taxed for unused property and today they no longer dot the countryside in farming areas.

We had about 20 acres of pastureland that ran along a dry gully 1/3 of a mile behind our house and ran the width of our farm. This pastureland was very heavily overgrown with trees, cactus, and bushes. It was so overgrown it served little purpose. There were only cow trails that ran through it, making it difficult to even find cows when they decided to venture into the wooded areas. So Dad decided to have it cleared. It was fun to watch the big D8 Caterpillar bulldozer knock down the trees and undergrowth and push everything into piles where they could be burned. I had never before gotten to watch anything quite as powerful as that Caterpillar work.

Once the land was cleared the entire pasture was planted in Coastal Bermuda grass, which grows to be about a foot tall. Cows graze on it year around and it is great for slowing rain runoff and reducing erosion. The Coastal Bermuda is still there today.

About every 10 years the stock tanks would fill up with silt and Dad had to hire a dragline to come out and dredge bucket after big bucket of mud out of the bottom of the tank in order to re-deepen it. The dragline was another huge machine that made quite an impression on this little boy.

Yet another neat machine was one that Dad bought to build terraces. In order to keep heavy rains from washing away the rich topsoil, many farmers would build terraces that were pretty much perpendicular to the direction the water flowed downhill. The terraces acted like a mini levee but were sloped downhill a couple of inches per 100 feet to allow for slow drainage rather than rapid runoff, thus greatly slowing erosion.

The terracing machine had a vertical auger that spun very fast with a shield on one side so it only flung the dirt in one direction building a low levee after several passes. Once Dad built all of the terraces he needed on our farm, he hired out to build terraces for other farmers during the winter months. Many of these soil conservation practices were subsidized by the U. S. Department of Agriculture.

Before we had a shredder for cutting stalks, after we harvested various crops, we used a two-row stalk cutter that was pulled by a small tractor. It had four heavy blades that were each about seven feet long and ran the full width of the implement. The blades were assembled in a seven-foot wide X shape, with each blade facing out. As the stalk cutter was pulled forward it hopped from one blade to the next and each time the next blade landed it chopped off anything in its seven-foot wide path.

One year a smooth talking salesman talked a lot of the farmers near Rosebud into planting popcorn. I think Dad planted about 150 acres but most of it did not sprout. When quite a bit of the seed did not come up we said we did not have a "good stand."

As soon as Dad saw that he would not have a successful popcorn crop because he had a bad stand, he plowed up all but about 20 acres (that did have a decent stand of popcorn) and replanted regular corn. When Dad harvested the remaining 20 acres of popcorn, the granary in town shelled it and loaded it onto a big truck that was built like a moving van. Dad laughed because pictures of fluffy popcorn were painted on the side of the trailer that made you think the popcorn was light even though the load of shelled popcorn kernels thoroughly exceeded state load limits.

When it became obvious that there was going to be a crop failure we would say that crop was not going "to make." But just because corn wasn't going to make did not necessarily mean that cotton wasn't going to make either. Cotton took a lot less water and matured later. Sometimes there were things you could do to soften the blow of a crop that failed. One year, when it became obvious that it was too late for a rain to save the corn crop, Dad decided to make "silage" (also referred to as "ensilage") for cattle feed rather than just let the corn wither and die.

First he put the dozer blade (like the blade on a Caterpillar bulldozer only much smaller) on the front of the biggest tractor he had and dug a trench about 4 feet deep and a little wider than the pickup. The trench sloped down a moderate hill for drainage. He hired the Hensons (remember we got Sally from Mr. Henson) to come in with a machine that cut the corn down, stalk and all, and mulched it into small pieces called ensilage.

It was hauled to the trench, dumped in and packed down by driving the tractor back and forth over it. When Dad was ready to feed the cows we backed the pickup up into the bottom of the trench and used a seed fork to load the wet silage and take it to troughs to feed it to the cows. The top few inches rotted and had to be thrown away but what was left was kind of like a very large wet salad. I was in about the 8th grade and feeding the cows was sometime my job, especially on weekends. Cows loved ensilage but it did not smell very good to this human nose.

One key source of information about farming was the local cotton ginner, Clarence Wolf. Clarence was a young go-getter and ready to share any knowledge he had. He would even come out to our farm and help Dad look for insects like boll weevils and bollworms. And he did it for free. Clarence really liked people and he enjoyed being around and helping farmers. There were times that we ate supper late because Dad was waiting for Clarence to come out and help him make decisions about when and what insecticide we should use to spray the cotton.

All farmers knew that you planted grain crops like corn and maize much earlier in the spring than you planted cotton. So one day Dad was out planting corn in the early spring when a neighbor who had a very small farm next to ours stopped by and asked him what he was planting. Thinking he was just pulling the guys leg, Dad said he was planting cotton. It was so absurd it never occurred to him that anyone wouldn't know he was just joking.

But that afternoon Dad noticed the neighbor out planting and to his horror figured out the neighbor was planting cotton. Cotton wouldn't come up until the ground warmed up several more degrees. That is all of that story that I remember. I don't know if Dad tried to stop him or not. But it is a clear example of the respect that farmer had for Emil Skupin's farming techniques.

Since there were tens of thousands of farmers nationally growing the same crops, there was no reason to keep secrets from each other. In practice the farmers all shared ideas and learned from each other. Sometimes you listened and learned innovative approaches. Often, all Dad had to do was just watch and "see what not to do."

One of the major problems that farmers and ranchers encountered regularly was screwworms infecting sores of the farm animals. I always dreaded helping Dad treat the infected cows and calves. Usually the worms were in the navel of a calf, but sometime they would infest a simple cut. A cow with pinkeye would occasionally get infected by screwworms and also have to be treated.

After Dad roped the calf we would tie his feet together and sit on the calf to hold him down while Dad treated the sore. These sores were ugly! The infected area might have hundreds of tiny screwworms in it that were eating the animal's "flesh." Dad would pour medicine into the wound to kill the screwworms and then dig out those on top with a stick. That seems weird today with all of the attention to cleanliness.

But he would just pick up a small limb, break it off, and start digging the worms out of the wound. He would have to repeat this procedure several times during one treatment to get the medicine all the way down to the bottom of the wound and kill all of the screwworms.

The problem was severe enough that the government developed a plan to eradicate screwworms back about the time I left home. Each farmer and rancher was asked for a donation to help fund the program. It was suggested they each donate about as much as treating their animals for screwworm for one year cost them and I think Dad donated about $150. Small boxes of sterile flies were dropped all over the countryside and soon the screwworms problem just ceased to exist.

If we did have an animal get infected after that we could place a small sample of the screwworms in a vial that was readily available and send it to Austin. A few days later a small airplane would drop a box or two of sterile flies on our farm and once again we would not have screwworms. I thought this program was an amazing success. But those sores with all of those little worms in them—they were one of the nastiest things I remember seeing on the farm!

One more farming story that shows Dad's farming innovation is that after my junior year at A&M he decided the 65 acre field in front of our house was not producing the crop yields he wanted and he was going to plant it in clover. Clover has nitrogen nodules on its roots and is a terrific fertilizer if you let it grow to full height and then just plowed it under while it was still green. The land would produce considerably better crops for years to come.

But instead of growing to two feet high, this clover grew to about five feet high and was loaded with seed from top to bottom so Dad decided to let it mature and combine it for the seed. I was sent out into the field with a hoe to cut down the sunflowers because they were so big they might damage the combine. There weren't that many sunflowers but 65 acres is a bit daunting for a single person to tackle.

The following week I had to go to ROTC summer camp in Waco. One of the side benefits of Air Force ROTC camp was we each got a solo ride in the cockpit with an Air Force pilot. I went up in a T33 jet trainer with an Air Force major who asked me where I would like to go. I said I would like to fly down to Rosebud and circle our farm. That was about 45 miles away and he said, "Sure, we can do that."

We made several passes over the farm and Dad was out combining that field of clover that day. Dad said he looked up and saw the plane and wondered if I wasn't in it. On the way back to the Air Force Base we did several dives where we experienced about 3 G's of force as we pulled back up out of each dive. I just barely made it back to base without loosing my lunch. Oh yes, clover seed brought a good price that year and Dad made a killing on the clover patch. And the land still got quite a bit of the benefit of having been planted in clover.

After high school I followed my older brother 60 miles down the road to Aggieland. Towards the end of my sophomore year in college I needed a birth certificate because I was in ROTC preparing to be an officer and a pilot in the US Air Force. When I got my birth certificate from the courthouse I found out that my middle name was not on it. My parents did not decide on my middle name, Charles, until several weeks after the birth certificate had already been filed. Fortunately, Dr. Sweptson, who delivered me 20 years earlier out in that rural farmhouse, was still practicing medicine in Rosebud so it wasn't hard to get the certificate amended.

Incidentally, the doctor's name was "Happy Jack" Sweptson. He owned the hospital and practiced medicine in Rosebud his entire life. Dr. Sweptson was probably the most respected man I have ever come across. My friend's mother, Julia McCollum, was going to name her son after him so he wanted her to name him Happy Jack. But she settled on "Jackie" instead. Shortly after I got out of college in the late 60's or early 70's the government condemned Dr Sweptson's hospital and the Ocker Rest home where Grandpa lived after his stroke because both buildings were wood structures and considered fire hazards.

The first time I ever sat in a dentist chair was when I took a physical to get into the Advanced Air Force ROTC program during the second semester of my sophomore year of college. Today, at the age of 65, I still have all 32 teeth and only 3 small cavities. The well water we drank on the farm, before it was contaminated with gasoline, was clearly responsible for my strong teeth.

Early in my junior year of college, Time Magazine published an extremely negative article about Texas A&M. I believe the writer was a long haired liberal hippy from the University of Texas who had taught one year at A&M and hated the conservative (read that as clean cut) military attitude that Aggies cherish and UT faculty doesn't.

It just so happened that Time Magazine had also written an article just a few months earlier about how life in small town America was dying. One of the six towns covered in the article was Rosebud, Texas. They noted that Rosebud had two funeral homes, two florists, and two old age homes and they quoted a local citizen who said, "Rosebud is Rotting."

Well, my Squadron 4 buddies decided it was required that "I" write a letter to the editor of Times Magazine. Of course the letter was a group project. You might even say they wrote the whole thing. Our primary goal was to get our letter printed in the letters to the editors' section of the magazine so it had to be short and clever. And we wanted to take a poke back at Time Magazine. This is as close as I can remember the wording of the letter:

> I am a junior at Texas A&M from Rosebud, Texas. Last summer you
> wrote an article about how small town life in America is dying and in it
> you said, "Rosebud is rotting." Last week you wrote a very negative

article putting down Texas A&M. But then I am a Democrat, and I suppose I should be glad you don't know the name of my girlfriend.

We had just thrown the "but then I'm a Democrat" in to gig Time Magazine because they were so obviously Republican and when my letter was published the editors left out those five words. That tiny short letter to the editor was posted on bulletin boards across the University. Hey, I had already used up my 15 minutes of fame before there even was such a thing.

Country Boy Observation: Want to know how to spot a product's weakness before you buy it? Listen to their ads. Whatever they tell you is their product's strength often turns out to be its weakness. For example: A satellite TV company says you can avoid those annoying cable outages with satellite. Yet they go down 99 times for every cable outage. And they tell you what to look out for right in their own ads.

David's 8 Row Combine
25 Feet Wide - 2007

History Lesson #20.
David—Still Farming

David farms almost twice as much land as Dad did without even a single helper most of the year. A bumper corn crop for Dad in the late 1950's, when he already used hybrid seed and fertilized heavily, was about 40 to 45 bushels per acre. I find it amazing that with advances in seeds and fertilizer a bumper crop on the same land now produces up to 120 bushels per acre. Parallel advances in farm machinery have allowed David to farm all of that land almost single handedly. He has some huge machinery!

Let me give you an example of current farming practices. Today David deals in the futures markets. Before he even plants, he sells most of his crop on the futures exchanges (with point of delivery being David's corn patch.) This assures him of a set price come harvest time. Having the broker accept delivery in David's corn patch means the buyer must provide the empty trucks for him to load in the cornfield right where he is harvesting.

David will call his broker and say he will be ready to harvest on Tuesday at 10:00 AM, for example, and he will need ten 18 wheelers a day. (You can't start harvesting early in the morning because you must wait for the dew to dry, otherwise the buyer will dock the farmer a percentage of the price he is to receive because the buyer will have to process the damp grain through a dryer in order to prevent the damp grain from rotting.)

David's combine gathers eight rows of corn at a time, shells the grain off of the corn cob, and augers the shelled corn up to where it will drop into a large bin on his combine, which does not take long to fill. He travels at a fast enough pace that you would have to trot quickly in order to keep up with the combine.

After about two round trips to the other end of the cornfield and back (called two rounds) he will have harvested 32 rows of corn and the bin will start to get full. He will then use his CB to radio his helper, (maybe his daughter, Lisa, who is a high school coach during the school year) and she will drive a tractor pulling a separate larger bin on wheels next to the combine and without stopping David will flip a lever and empty his bin full of shelled corn into the "auxiliary" bin pulled by a tractor. The helper driving the tractor must stay beside the combine so David can use another lever to position his auger so the grain will fall where there is space for it in the auxiliary bin.

After David dumps two full combine bins into the larger auxiliary bin, the helper must go to the edge of the field and empty the load into the 18-wheeler while David keeps harvesting. After David finishes gathering his crop he can use his combine to work out for the public, i.e., hire out to harvest other farmers' grain crops. If you think a Hummer is really expensive you should check out that combine. He paid $80,000 for it second hand and he probably uses it less than six weeks a year.

David is a great welder. Farmers often need to repair farm machinery and they can ill afford to wait several days to get a part repaired every time one breaks. Dad used to worry and fret every time he had to wait for the blacksmith, Chris Davis, to fix a broken part. David can usually do the job in minutes. In addition to minor repairs he has also done some pretty complicated jobs. About 15 years ago his helper was moving the grain truck in the corn patch where David was combining and a corn stalk got stuck behind the muffler and caught the truck on fire. David had an extinguisher on the combine but before he could get there and put the fire out, the cab of the truck had burned to a crisp.

David noticed that the motor, truck frame, and the steel bed on the burned truck were still in good shape. So that winter he found the same make of truck in a junkyard and bought it for parts. He used his cutting torch to remove the burned out truck cab from the frame and installed (as in welded) the cab from the truck he had bought onto his truck frame where the burned cab had been.

That is correct, cab, seat, dash, instrument panel, clutch and brake petals, cab flooring, and all. Of course he had to completely rewire the truck's electrical system, replace the front tires, brakes, battery, and stuff like that. When he got through he painted the cab a cherry red. No, he didn't hire someone to paint the cab cherry red. David, and the farm hand that worked for him at the time, did the entire project by themselves. No one would have ever suspected the kind of fire the truck had been through because it looked like a brand new truck when they finished.

I have another story about David and his welding prowess that took place back in the early 1970's that I want to tell you. Back then farmers were just beginning to convert from four row equipment to six row equipment. It would save a lot of labor, gasoline, and allow David to farm more land if he could plant and cultivate six rows at a time instead of four rows. If you plant six rows at a time all of your implements have to do six rows at a time or misaligned rows will be accidentally be plowed up when you cultivate with a different number of rows than you planted with. And the conversion to six row equipment isn't cheap.

David bought an old two row cultivator at the junkyard for next to nothing and welded one row to the both ends of his existing four row cultivator. Wow—Two rows plus one on the right side of his tractor is three rows. And two row plus one on the left side of his tractor is three. Now he had a six row cultivator.

But it isn't quite as easy as David made it look. There is a lot of stress way out on the end of a farm implement like a cultivator and it will break down and you will just have a pile of junk when you need it most if it is not adequately reinforced. Of course David added the necessary steel to make it a successful conversion and he used it for years until he converted to eight row equipment.

Country Boy Observation: Drug companies are lobbing congress to outlaw the use of supplements without a prescription. I used a nutritionist and lowered my bad cholesterol (LDL) by 90 units (48%) in 40 days using a supplement! This legislation is not about what is best for the people. Watch what you ask for. You might get it.

Henry at Air Force ROTC Summer Camp - 1963

Conclusion

We usually think of history as something that happened a long, long time ago. I hope people my age can share my experiences along with their own with their grandchildren as a history lesson about our generation. Not of something that happened centuries ago, but of things that happened to us at a time in which huge changes were taking place so rapidly that children today have no personal experiences that relate to their grandparents' childhood experiences. Grandparents who have a few stories about their parents childhood might pass along those memories to their grandchildren also.

I think for those of you who are my age and grew up in town, my experiences will trigger memories of your own that are just as different from today as my experiences were. None of us had central heat and air, TV, or computers and we all had to find ways to entertain ourselves. My hope is that adults will share this book with their children and grandchildren and then talk about their own experiences that were, oh so different from today, not really so very long ago. Even things that happened in our lifetime are now history and played an important part in molding us, our families, our relationships, and even our nation.

My life as a child was definitely not "all work and no play." Much of the work I have described took place when school was out for the summer. I never did the important farm jobs. Sure I drove tractors to cut stalks and rolled (remember the roller packed the soil over the newly planted seed), but I never bedded the land to lay out the straight rows, I never planted anything, and I never cultivated. Dad, or maybe one of the full time people he hired to help him do farm labor, did those major jobs.

No one but Dad drove the combine until several years after David returned to the farm. The investment was just too great to put anyone else behind the wheel of his combines. Until my junior year in high school I had perfect attendance at school most years. I probably stayed home and helped Dad in a pinch about two days a year the last two years in high school. Although my dad did not complete junior high, it was obvious that both of my parents thought education was essential.

I had chores to do when I got home from school but my parents let me play high school football in the fall and I ran track in the spring. I wasn't a very good player, but the guys on the team were the group of people I wanted as friends, and that required two-a-day football practices the two weeks before school started and practice after school each day. Obviously playing football was time spent not working on the farm.

There were times as when Dad was planting crops that I might have to get on a tractor and roll after school or do a few other small jobs like that. The work I was required to do was light compared to what many of my friends who lived on farms did. For example, they may have hauled a lot more hay and picked more cotton than I did. Mom and Dad were very proud that they were able to send all three of us boys to college and we didn't have to work while we were in school. Well, not unless we made the mistake of going home for the weekend, which often meant we were given the opportunity to spend some time on a tractor.

Note I never actually went into the military. I was number one in my ROTC outfit at summer camp after my junior year in college and I graduated "Distinguished Military Student" (I didn't see either of those coming.) But I had a car wreck the day before I was to go back to A&M for my senior year, lost my pilot's contract because I had been unconscious and might have suffered brain damage, and thus I never got to go to Viet Nam. That car wreck turned out to be a major turning point in my life.

One thing that I did find interesting about school was that my grades would go down and then get better and better after each transition. I made straight A's the last semester at every level. That included the 5th grade, the 8th grade, the 12th grade and my senior year in college. And I never came close to those kinds of grades any other time. Ok, so why would good grades be important when I was a senior? As a high school senior I was surprised to suddenly find myself qualified for the National Honor Society and to be the 13th and last (in a class of 33 students) who graduated with honors. That didn't hurt when I applied to Texas A&M.

All A's my last semester in college had a lot to do with my getting hired by Texaco so the importance there is self-evident. When I went to be interviewed at Texaco I didn't point out that I had "cheated" a bit to make all A's that last semester by taking four senior level Math courses and a senior level Physics course. I suspect that a lot of you also loaded up on easy grade point courses your last semester in college.

Anybody can make good grades if they don't have to take hard courses like English, history, economics, business, education or other stuff like that. Courses that depend on being good at reading and writing are especially difficult for those of us who are dyslexic. Teachers were always saying we could do better if we just tried harder. I'm here to tell you, it ain't that simple folks. If it were, the people who make good grades in English would also make good grades in Math and Physics if they just tried harder. How is it I've never heard a teacher make that suggestion?

Even though I am a bit embarrassed that I am not more proficient in my use of the English language, I believe that Mrs. Stubbs and Miss Pendergrass, my high school English teachers, would give me an A for the effort I've put into writing this book.

I graduated from college and got a job with Texaco programming computers in 1964. Computers were very, very new then. They were massive and even big corporations only had one or two. PCs would not exist for another 20 years. When PCs were invented in 1984 (You gotta be kidding—no PC's before 1984?) they still didn't do anything compared to today's computers. And PC's certainly did not communicate with other computers when they were first introduced.

I remember attending a management class when I worked for Texaco where the instructor pointed out there would never be the number of cars that General Motors was projecting for the future because there wouldn't be a place to park them all. But the instructor did not envision a multistory parking garage. Someone probably built the very first one in the 1970's.

When I was a youngster back in the early 50's there were no TVs, no cell phones, nothing with a computer chip in it, no power steering, automatic transmission or air conditioning on cars, no freeways, no air conditioning in homes, no microwaves, no ice makers, no clothes dryers, no satellites, no cell phones, no cordless phones, no push button phones, we could not even get a telephone, ... The list of things we take for granted today that did not exist in the country back then is endless. Like I said, "the times, they were a changing." We did not feel deprived by all of these things that we did not have because, like the instructor in the management class, we couldn't even envision the things that would become common in our lifetime.

I still remember my wife coming home from the wedding shower that was given for her in Rosebud before we got married. All of the ladies stood and introduced themselves. They gave their name, how they knew me, and where they were from (Aunt Tillie from Travis, for instance). Anne expected everybody to be from either Rosebud or Cameron. But almost no one was. They were from the rural communities of Briary, Clarkson, Jones Prairie, Baileyville, Silver City, Walker's Creek, Wilderville, Travis, Burlington, Ben Arnold, etc. She didn't have a clue where any of those places were, even though they were almost all within about 12 miles of the shower they were holding for her. Don't bother looking for them on a map. You won't find most of them. Many, like Briary, have a population of zero today.

In closing let me ask you one question. Wouldn't it have been neat to grow up on a farm and go to a small high school 50 years ago? Wait, wait, wait, before you answer no—Would you have liked to be able to play outside endlessly with minimal adult supervision at the age of five? Would you have liked to be encouraged to hitchhike six miles each way to and from Little League baseball in order to do something you wanted to do? Would you have liked to contribute to your families' financial well being by driving mules over newly planted crops or going with your dad and helping tie up hay bales at the age of seven? What would you think if they turned out the lights at the ball field and everyone just went home and left you standing on the corner under a street light at 9:00 PM at the age of 11? Does that sound outlandish to you? It really wasn't back then. Would you have enjoyed driving a tractor and hauling the entire family corn crop to market at the age of 13? Let me tell you, I was one proud kid as I drove that tractor hauling the crop through town several times each day! We are talking about independence, responsibility and trust at a young age that children today cannot imagine. I feel there has to be a lot of good in that mix somewhere!

> Y'all be good now, ya hear. And drive careful. That's what my parents always said when we left Rosebud. If it was good enough for them back then it is good enough for me now.

Post Script

Be careful what you do or say because you never know who is watching. This story is about something that happened in my sophomore year at Texas A&M.

I may not have been a very good athlete but I did play football in junior high and high school. Rosebud High had such a limited number of athletes that by my senior year I actually played at least half of each game and sometimes quite a bit more. To put that into perspective, I had four different classmates that lettered as freshmen and I did not letter until I was a senior. But even though I served mostly as a tackling dummy those first three years in high school the athletes were the group I wanted to be a part of.

Patrick James was in the class behind me and he reminded me a lot of myself. Just like I hadn't, he didn't get into any games as an underclassman either. After high school Patrick decided to come to Texas A&M. One Sunday afternoon in the spring of his freshman year he had a nasty one-car accident while driving back to A&M. I was told he was driving too fast and missed a curve.

The first person to come by the accident just happened to be Dr. Sweptson but he was unable to save Patrick and he died there that day. I put on my dress military uniform and along with a few Aggies from his ROTC unit I drove the 60 miles to Rosebud to Patrick's funeral. There he was in the casket in his freshman ROTC uniform. The freshman uniform is kind of plain but it looked plenty special on him that day.

At the funeral Patrick's dad told my dad that Patrick had looked up to me and had gone to A&M because I had gone there. You could have blown me away. Wow, how overwhelmed I felt! I doubt if many of us, as a 19 year old, think of ourselves as a role model for someone else. **For Patrick—Gig-um Aggies**

David, Henry and Robert

What happened to the Skupin Boys

The Skupin boys all got college degrees, we all married women with college degrees, and we are all still married to our original wives. We each have a son and a daughter, and we are all proud of our parents, our wives, our children and of each other.

Robert got a degree in Mechanical Engineering from Texas A&M, and after serving in the Air Force, worked his entire career in many different locations around the nation for United States Gypsum. He was plant manager at the largest gypsum plant in the world in Sweetwater, Texas before finishing his career at the USG company headquarters in Chicago. Their brand name for gypsum board was "Sheetrock." He and Janis have retired to a community east of Gainesville, Texas where Janis tends to her horses and rides them regularly and Robert works on their land, rides some with Janis and plays golf. They both keep themselves very busy.

David got a degree in Industrial Engineering from North Texas State and after teaching high school shop for a couple of years, returned to Rosebud and today is still running the expanded family farm. He has used his mechanical and welding skills to restore a couple of cars (during the winters) and he always seems to have a couple of projects in the mill. His wife Sharon went back to school at Baylor while teaching and earned a Masters degree in reading for learning disabled children. She has taught at every level from kindergarten through high school, and has also taught in men's, women's, and the juvenile prison systems.

I got a degree in Mathematics from Texas A&M and worked for Texaco for 29 years (where I met my wife, Anne, who was also working as a programmer at the time.) I spent most of my career managing and programming geophysical seismic applications, although the last few years I worked in middle management in various different computer functions.

Following that I worked for 8 years as a Financial Advisor for Morgan Stanley Dean Witter.

We have lived in Houston, New Orleans, Tulsa and are now retired back in Houston. I have a regular golf game scheduled three times a week, though I don't mind playing a little more if the opportunity arises. While raising our two children, Anne became interested in Art and studied at the Museum of Fine Arts School (The Glassel School) here in Houston. In Tulsa she went to the University of Tulsa and earned her Master of Fine Arts in sculpture. Today she teaches part time at a privately owned art school for children.

We all are involved and supportive of our children, grandchildren and their lives. Probably the one thing the Skupin boys share the most in common is we all married very capable women. They are distinctly different from each other, I grant you, but all three are incredible women.

Country Boy Observation: Most Republicans I know seem to believe they don't know a single American that is stupid enough to vote Democrat, even though on average, the Democrats have gotten more votes in the last four presidential elections than the Republicans. Go figure …

978-0-595-44047-4
0-595-44047-9

LaVergne, TN USA
08 December 2010
207800LV00004B/4/A